Philadelphia's Haunted
HISTORIC WALKING TOUR

CYNTHIA BRACELIN

4880 Lower Valley Road • Atglen, PA 19310

Other Schiffer Books on Related Subjects:
Spooky York, Pennsylvania. Scott D. Butcher and Dinah Roseberry
ISBN: 978-0-7643-3021-6.

Boston's Haunted History: Exploring the Ghosts and Graves of Beantown. Christopher Forest.
ISBN: 978-0-7643-2874-9.

Arizona's Haunted Hotspots. Heather Woodward.
ISBN: 978-0-7643-3748-2.

Type set in Adobe Caslon Pro

ISBN: 978-0-7643-4437-4
Printed in The United States of America

Published by Schiffer Publishing, Ltd.
4880 Lower Valley Road
Atglen, PA 19310
Phone: (610) 593-1777; Fax: (610) 593-2002
E-mail: Info@schifferbooks.com

For our complete selection of fine books on this and related subjects, please visit our website at www.schifferbooks.com. You may also write for a free catalog.

This book may be purchased from the publisher. Please try your bookstore first.

We are always looking for people to write books on new and related subjects. If you have an idea for a book, please contact us at proposals@schifferbooks.com

Schiffer Publishing's titles are available at special discounts for bulk purchases for sales promotions or premiums. Special editions, including personalized covers, corporate imprints, and excerpts can be created in large quantities for special needs. For more information, contact the publisher.

Dedication

For my saintly parents, Grace and Jim.
They always knew I had this in me.

Acknowledgments

A million thanks to my dear friends Kathy and Brian, who helped and supported me every step of the way. Thanks to Brian for feeding the "starving artist," and thanks to Kathy for feeding the "starving artist's dog." I would like to thank Dinah Roseberry and Schiffer Publishing for believing in me and giving me the amazing opportunity to write this book. I would also like to thank The Free Library of Philadelphia just for being there and always available, day and night. Finally, thanks to everyone I interviewed and for sharing their unique stories with me. I loved every minute of the research and am so grateful to have had the opportunity to share this with you.

Contents

Foreword

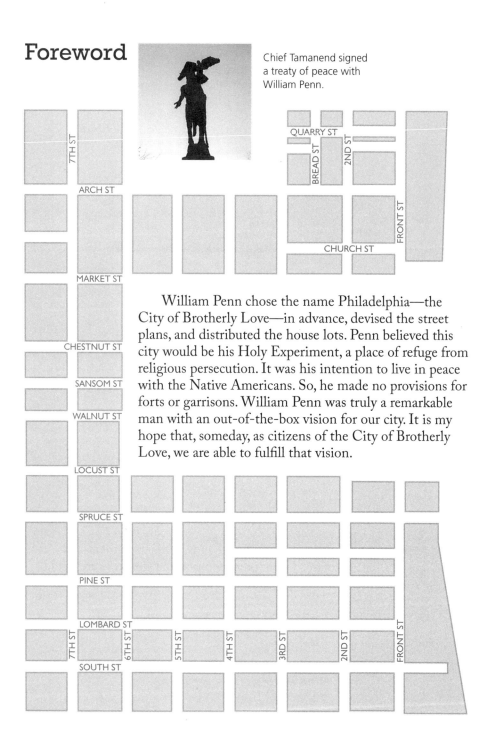

Chief Tamanend signed a treaty of peace with William Penn.

William Penn chose the name Philadelphia—the City of Brotherly Love—in advance, devised the street plans, and distributed the house lots. Penn believed this city would be his Holy Experiment, a place of refuge from religious persecution. It was his intention to live in peace with the Native Americans. So, he made no provisions for forts or garrisons. William Penn was truly a remarkable man with an out-of-the-box vision for our city. It is my hope that, someday, as citizens of the City of Brotherly Love, we are able to fulfill that vision.

Introduction

"Midnight to one belongs to the dead. Good Lord, deliver us."
– The Fog, dir. John Carpenter, written in a diary found buried
in the wall of a church.

There are many recurring themes among the ghost stories in this area of the country. There are also many reasons for a spirit to return from the dead. Some deceased individuals want or need to contact the living, and some poor souls are trapped between the two worlds, forced to relive a trauma over and over again.

The most obvious reason for this is the Revolutionary War. Young men from all over enlisted to fight in the Continental Army with General Washington. While these men were able bodied, they were not soldiers by any means.

Then, there was an invasion of young British and Hessian soldiers, all filled with passion and strong political convictions, fighting for their countries. Many Patriots, British, and Hessian soldiers perished in battle. None of the dead returned home to their families. Washington Square is just one place in which these dead soldiers are buried in the ground. The British and Hessians died on a foreign land, away from the ones they loved.

While some Patriot soldiers remain unidentified, they are not forgotten. We will always remember the sacrifice the unknown soldier made for his country. Such raw emotional resonance never dies. It is only channeled and, eventually, released. This is why there are still sightings of Revolutionary War soldiers. Some may be trying to find their way home and some may still be fighting the Revolutionary War.

Another extremely popular reason is love. Love and war were intertwined. Many women awaited the return of their husbands, brothers, fathers, and beloved ones. When these men did not return home, the women were left to raise the children and survive in the new nation on their own. The intensity of their love and emotion did not die with their men. It only grew stronger. War also brings us tales of unrequited love, which never end on a happy note; they usually end with murder, suicide, or both.

Then, we have sightings of the ghostly lover who was wronged. Philadelphia has been the setting for countless love stories of all types, good and bad, and still remains the City of Brotherly Love.

Whether it be unrequited love, star-crossed lovers, or even the eternal love of families destroyed by war, Philadelphia has endured all of it and survived to become one of the most haunted cities in America.

Colonial Time Line
of the City of Philadelphia

1682	William Penn, aboard the ship *Welcome* lands in New Castle, Delaware. Penn travels up to the land between the Delaware and Schuylkill Rivers in a row boat. He names the land Philadelphia, City of Brotherly Love.
1701	William Penn returns to England for the final time.
1718	William Penn dies in England.
1723	Benjamin Franklin arrives in Philadelphia from Boston, at the age of 16.
1745	Market stalls were built in Second Street, between Pine and Lombard Streets. Head House Square is born.
1748	The Philadelphia Dancing Assembly Annual Ball takes place. This is the beginning of Philadelphia High Society.
1749	The first theater company opens in the colonies.
1752	Benjamin Franklin performs his famous kite experiment, proving lightning is a form of electricity. He does this in the area of 10th and Ludlow Streets, which is now St. Stephen's Episcopal Church.
1755	Benjamin Franklin opens the first hospital at Eighth and Spruce Streets. Pennsylvania Hospital still treats the sick citizens of Philadelphia today, just as in Colonial Days.
1765	Mass protests in the city on the news of English Parliament's Stamp Act. A boycott of imported (British) goods was strongly requested of the citizens of Philadelphia.
1774	First Continental Congress is held in the Pennsylvania State House, also known as Independence Hall.
1776	The Declaration of Independence was debated on July 2nd and signed on July 4th in the Assembly Room of the Pennsylvania State House.
1777	General Howe's army marches north from Maryland to take Germantown on October 4th. The British occupy the city of Philadelphia shortly after. Members of the Continental Congress take the Liberty Bell and seek refuge in Lancaster, Pennsylvania.
1778	The British Army leaves Philadelphia in order to move on to New York City.
1780	Pennsylvania becomes the first state to abolish slavery, calling for emancipation by the year 1827.
1782	The Bank of North America, a.k.a. First Bank of the United States, opens on the corner of 3rd and Chestnut Streets, under the direction of Alexander Hamilton.
1787	The Constitutional Convention meets in the Pennsylvania State House, also known as Independence Hall.
1780	Philadelphia is the Capital of the United States for ten years until 1790.

CHAPTER I

THE WALKING TOUR

If you are visiting Philadelphia for the first time, the Independence Visitor's Center should be your first stop. Independence Hall requires date/time stamped tickets for admission to the building and includes a formal tour with one of the park rangers, who are absolutely fabulous and assist you with your every need. The tickets are free and you can obtain them at the Visitor's Center. You definitely want to pick these up first thing in the morning, as there are a limited number of tickets for each tour. You can sign up for tours of the Bishop White and Todd Houses, if you wish. The house tours are also free, but only offered Wednesday through Sunday and at limited times.

The Independence Visitor's Center is located at 6th and Market Streets, where the park rangers provide you with tickets and literature. Once you obtain your tickets, cross Market Street at 6th street. From there, you can walk through Liberty Bell Plaza and arrive across the street from Independence Hall. Allow for extra time because you must pass through a security screening before entering the grounds of Independence Hall: fifteen minutes should be sufficient. Also, be prepared to empty all purses, backpacks, etc.

After you obtain your tickets and pass through security, we will begin our walking tour here at Independence Hall. This is the best place to begin—where Liberty itself began!

Philadelphia Haunted Historic

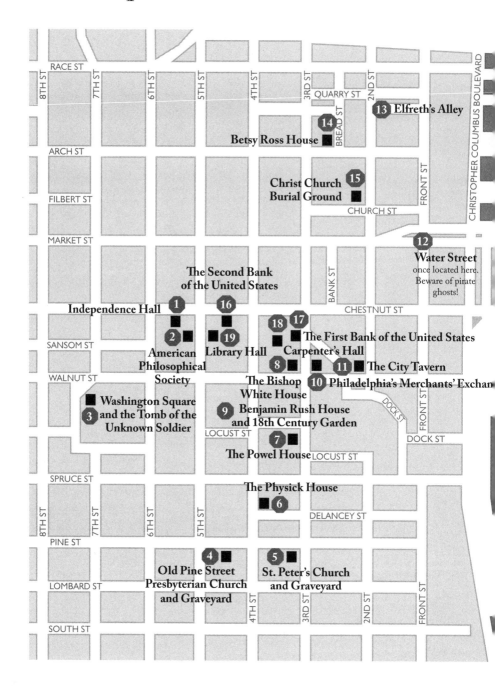

RACE ST

8TH ST
7TH ST
6TH ST
5TH ST
4TH ST
3RD ST
QUARRY ST
2ND ST

13 **Elfreth's Alley**

14

Betsy Ross House ■

ARCH ST

FILBERT ST

Christ Church **15**
Burial Ground ■

CHURCH ST

FRONT ST

CHRISTOPHER COLUMBUS BOULEVARD

MARKET ST

12

Water Street
once located here.
Beware of pirate
ghosts!

The Second Bank
of the United States

BANK ST

CHESTNUT ST

Independence Hall **1**
■

16
■

SANSOM ST

2 ■ ■ **19**
American Library Hall
Philosophical
Society

18 **17**
■ ■
The First Bank of the United States

Carpenter's Hall

8 ■ ■ **11** ■ **The City Tavern**

WALNUT ST

The Bishop **10** Philadelphia's Merchants' Exchan
White House

■ Washington Square
3 and the Tomb of the
Unknown Soldier

9 Benjamin Rush House
and 18th Century Garden

LOCUST ST

DOCK ST

FRONT ST

7 ■
The Powel House LOCUST ST

DOCK ST

SPRUCE ST

The Physick House
■ **6**

8TH ST
7TH ST
6TH ST
5TH ST

DELANCEY ST

PINE ST

4 ■
Old Pine Street
Presbyterian Church
and Graveyard

5 ■
St. Peter's Church
and Graveyard

LOMBARD ST

4TH ST
3RD ST
2ND ST
FRONT ST

SOUTH ST

Walking Tour Map

Part I:

*Haunted Locations in Old City
and Society Hill, with Corresponding Points
on the Tour Map*

1 INDEPENDENCE HALL

CHESTNUT STREET BETWEEN 5TH AND 6TH STREETS
OPEN DAILY, 9 – 5   FREE ADMISSION

It is often called the "Birthplace of Liberty"—maybe the best historical nickname ever! Independence Hall was originally called the Pennsylvania State House. Here, in the Assembly Room, on July 4, 1776, the Founding Fathers signed and adopted the Declaration of Independence. The Assembly Room itself has an impressive history.

1775	George Washington appointed Commander and Chief of the Continental Army
1776	July 4th, the Declaration signed and adopted
1777	The design of the American flag agreed upon
1778	The Articles of Confederation adopted
1787	The United States Constitution drafted

Here are three views of the Independence Hall Clock Tower. Take notice of the window, below the clock. In the first photo, the window is clear. However, in the second and third, a misty fog is visible.

This building has appeared in many films and television shows. One of my favorite scenes in the movie *National Treasure* shows Ben Gates (Nicholas Cage) climbing on the roof from the clock tower to find a pair of eye glasses hidden in the masonry of the building.

The entire building and adjoining grounds have been the source of a considerable amount of paranormal activity, which has been consistent throughout the years. Visitors have reported sightings of entities moving around the first floor of the Hall's central clock tower. Some manifestations have shown or revealed themselves in photos. The unsuspecting tourist, ghost hunter, or photographer realizes this after developing the film. They often capture these paranormal images in the window on the second floor. The entities responsible for them may be elusive, but they are definitely not camera shy!

Benjamin Franklin, who was extremely active in life, seems to be enjoying an active afterlife as well. There are recorded sightings of Mr. Franklin's ghost walking around in the building and outside on the Independence Hall grounds, much as he did more than two hundred years ago.

There have also been sightings of Benedict Arnold's ghost in Independence Hall (first floor). Arnold, or perhaps his ghost, may be trying to settle unresolved issues. Maybe his troubled spirit is remorseful over his treasonous behavior. His spirit may carry so much bitterness that he is forced to relive his treacherous actions here. As for now, it remains a mystery.

It's no surprise that sightings still occur here; it seems only logical that this place would remain spiritually active. When you combine our Founding Fathers' emotional intensity with their strong individual personalities, not to mention the history of the building itself, and add a large dose of revolution and rebellion, you've got the perfect recipe for paranormal activity.

Sometimes tragedies and intense emotions endow symbols with the power to give comfort, reassurance and strength. After 9-11, I remember the presence of The National Guard, along with the protective boarding around the Independence Hall compound, seriously altered the energy of the area, not just the aesthetic appearance of the building. Our entire country was enveloped in a horrendous, tumultuous energy, but that never really hit home with me until I saw Independence Hall covered in boards and surrounded by metal fencing and men with guns, protecting it. It was at that one significant moment that I realized how we truly lost our innocence—but not our grace.

My friend and I decided to take a haunted history tour a month or so after 9-11. This was the first time I had been in town since the attacks. We were not allowed to be on the side of the street where Independence Hall stood. The boards and metal fencing prohibited anyone from even standing on the corner of 5th and Chestnut Streets. We had to "observe" the grounds from a block away. While I fully understood the severity of the situation and sincerely appreciated the National Guard for protecting this sacred place, it was heartbreaking and stomach turning to see it in such a state. This building was a childhood friend, a landmark, a meeting place; home. Gone were the innocent days of cutting through the grounds to get from one block to the other. The mushroom cloud of energy coming from the protected compound was a combination of several powerful emotions, including a fierce protective instinct to keep this birthplace of our country safe, and contempt and pure hatred for those who wished to destroy it.

At the end of the day, the strongest energy I felt resonating from Independence Hall, even from a block away, was not hateful or contemptuous; ironically, it was a sentiment of survival. If buildings can speak, and, after that night, I honestly believe they can, that building spoke to me, directly to my heart, and it said, "I am here. I am Liberty, and I will be here forever to show everyone's children and their children's children what freedom and liberty are." Maybe Stephen King is right: some buildings "shine." If that is the case, then Independence Hall shines like a beacon. May this building shine forever and inspire all who visit.

View of the Scottish Monument, Front and Chestnut Streets.

"We hold these truths to be self-evident, that all men are created equal, that they are endowed by their Creator with certain unalienable Rights, that among these are Life, Liberty, and the pursuit of Happiness. That to secure these rights, Governments are instituted among Men, deriving their just powers from the consent of the governed. That whatever any Form of Government becomes destructive of these ends, it is the Right of the People to alter or abolish it, and to institute new Government, laying its foundation on such principles and organizing its powers in such form, as to them shall seem most likely to effect their Safety and Happiness."

– Thomas Jefferson, The Declaration of Independence, as adopted by Congress, 1776.

2 THE AMERICAN PHILOSOPHICAL SOCIETY

104 SOUTH 5TH STREET

OPEN APRIL – OCTOBER:
THURSDAY – SUNDAY, 10 – 4
and FIRST FRIDAYS UNTIL 8 PM

NOVEMBER – DECEMBER:
FRIDAY – SUNDAY, 10 – 4

DONATION REQUESTED
SEE MORE AT WWW.APSMUSEUM.ORG/VISIT

The American Philosophical Society (APS) is located only a few feet from Independence Hall. Benjamin Franklin founded it in 1743 to promote "useful knowledge." It is the oldest scholarly society in America. Among its most famous members are George Washington, Thomas Jefferson, the Marquis de Lafayette, Charles Darwin, Thomas Edison, Ralph Waldo Emerson, and Albert Einstein.

The plaque by the entrance, on the left wall, says, "Judson Daland, 1860-1937." According to two employees at APS, Mr. Daland is interred in the wall there. As it sounds like something from Edgar Allan Poe or Alfred Hitchcock, I am unsure of the validity of this claim. Both employees shared with me personal experiences they'd had in the building, which include sudden temperature changes, sightings of shadow figures on the upper floor, and a generally eerie feeling when alone inside. Others have reported sightings of Benjamin Franklin on the grounds near both the American Philosophical Society and Library Hall buildings.

SUPERNATURAL DATA: apparition

An apparition is a physical manifestation of a spirit or an entity. It can take many forms: transparent, mist-like, even solid living person. Most of the time, the apparition disappears very quickly after being seen by the living.

Exit the grounds of Independence Hall through the gate closest to the statue of Revolutionary War hero Commodore Barry.

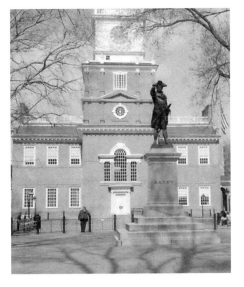

GHOST STORY: CURTIS PUBLISHING BUILDING

There are three interesting ghost stories related to the buildings in the area surrounding Independence Hall. In *Annals of Philadelphia*, John Watson describes a haunted house at Fifth and Walnut Streets:

"On the northeast corner of Walnut and Fifth Streets, once stood a house generally called 'the haunted house.' Because of Mr. B. having there killed his wife…it long remained empty for the dread of its invisible guest."
(Watson, Vol. 1, pp. 306-307)

The building across Walnut Street from this house is the Penn Mutual Building. It stands on the former site of the Walnut Street Prison. Many criminals were hanged here, including a pirate named Wilkinson. He was taken into custody after he murdered a man in Marcus Hook and killed three people in Delaware. After a failed attempt to escape, he was executed. Wilkinson is said to be one of the pirates who haunt the ever infamous, ever mysterious Water Street.

Across 6th Street from the Commodore Barry statue is the Curtis Publishing Building. It is famous for publishing the *Saturday Evening Post* and *Lady's Home Journal*. It is also known as the setting for a story of true love beyond the grave. In the eastern lobby is a mosaic entitled *Dream Garden*. It consists of 10,000 pieces of glass and was created by Tiffany & Company. Beneath the mosaic is a reflecting pool.

In 1972, a security guard named Leon Thompson was working in the Curtis Building. As part of his job, he interacted with many people who walked the halls of the Curtis and Penn Mutual Buildings, and became friendly with a man named John, who worked in the Curtis Building with Leon.

John met and fell in love with Sally, who worked across the street at Penn Mutual. They met near the mosaic on October 14th and got engaged exactly a year later, in front of the mosaic. Sally was so excited she fell into the reflecting pool. They were married a year later on October 14th, of course, and planned to honeymoon in Mexico, but, tragically, their plane crashed and no one survived.

According to Mr. Thompson's accounts, every year, on October 14th, for the duration of his employment at the Curtis Publishing Building, he could hear the sound of a woman's laughter near the reflecting pool. No one was ever anywhere near the mosaic when this happened. Could it have been John and Sally telling their friend they were together and happy on their special anniversary? Anything is possible in love—especially eternal love.

3 WASHINGTON SQUARE AND THE TOMB OF THE UNKNOWN SOLDIER OF THE REVOLUTIONARY WAR

**WASHINGTON SQUARE PARK,
ON WALNUT STREET,
BETWEEN 6TH AND 7TH STREETS**

As you exit the Independence Hall grounds near the statue of Commodore Barry, travel on 6th Street toward Walnut Street. Cross Walnut Street and enter Washington Square Park.

Washington Square served as a cemetery for 90 years, until late in the 18th century. More than 2,000 Revolutionary soldiers and prisoners of war were buried here. Eventually, it became a Potter's Field, like Logan Square. In late 1793, victims of the yellow fever epidemic were buried in mass graves in the square. In total, 10,000 bodies are buried here.

In a letter to his wife, Abigail, John Adams commented succinctly on the massive pits dug in Washington Square to bury the victims of the Yellow Fever epidemic when he said, "I never in my whole life was affected with so much melancholy."

Today, it contains the Tomb of the Unknown Soldier of the Revolutionary War, along with an Eternal Flame. At the center of the monument is George Washington in a life-sized likeness, but not the war general we think we know. Instead, he's at peace, with a walking stick in his hand, an older, wiser man, looking across the burial ground to Independence Hall. He seems to be contemplating the past, all the sacrifices made and the victories won. Passersby have reported sightings of Shadow People or Shadow Figures here. Most of the sightings occur near the Tomb of the Unknown Soldier.

Washington Square Monument, Tomb of the Unknown Soldier and the Eternal Flame.

SUPERNATURAL DATA: shadow figures

According to Raymond Buckland, Shadow People, Shadow figures, or Shadow Ghosts fall into one of the following three categories:

- They appear as a dark, misty shape hovering over the ground.
- They appear almost inside a dark, dense cloud like substance.
- They appear in human form and may be as tall as nine feet.

Shadow figures rarely have facial features or any other recognizable attributes, such as clothing style. They are more like human-sized silhouettes. Mr. Buckland also states that sometimes people find Shadow Figures frightening, not because of an ominous or threatening presence, but due to their dark appearance and possible lack of facial features.

Ghost Story: The Legend of Leah

In the early days of surgical medicine, grave robbing was a profitable endeavor. Obtaining corpses from a Potter's Field was rather easy and resulted in a quick sale to a physician and/or medical students for educational purposes.

A peculiar Quaker woman named Leah appointed herself guardian of the dead in Washington Square. Hunched over with age, she guarded the dead in the early morning hours, covered in a dark blanket, and never made eye contact with anyone. Her presence made the corpses-for-cash transactions nearly impossible. No one knew her true identity, but the legend was passed from generation to generation.

She eventually died, of course, which only proved to be a temporary setback to her perpetual guardianship over the graves. Pedestrians have reported sightings of her ghost over the years. The reports are always the same—a ghostly figure of a woman cloaked in a dark blanket, cape, or heavy cloth, hunched over and gliding between graves, acknowledging no one.

The most recent account of Leah was in 1994, by a Philadelphia Police Detective. He had stopped to transfer coffee to his traveling cup in the early morning hours. He saw what he thought was an "old bag lady" near Walnut Street. She seemed very strange. As he moved closer, he was shocked to discover she had no face or head under the blanket wrapped around her. Leah then vanished before his eyes.

SUPERNATURAL DATA: premature burial

People were occasionally buried alive due to catatonia and other organic diseases. Undertakers attached bells to a string and sealed the other end in coffins. The graveyard workers would patrol the cemetery several times a night, listening for the ringing of the bells. The term graveyard shift dates back to the 16th century.

Historical Data:
The British Occupation of Philadelphia

On September 26, 1777, British soldiers occupied the city of Philadelphia. In anticipation of their arrival, many patriots and businessmen fled the city. In a strange twist of events, General Washington's soldiers looted the city, taking anything that may have been useful to the British. Three quarters of the population who remained were women and children. Many of the remaining citizens were Loyalists, who were very anxious to see the British take over because they still perceived themselves as British citizens. When the British soldiers arrived, they occupied the some of the finest homes (i.e., mansions) they could find, and established a puppet government. Churches were turned into hospitals for the wounded British soldiers who fought in the Battles of Brandywine and Germantown. The British Navy succeeded in blockading American ports, keeping all goods and supplies from reaching the city. The British remained in the City of Philadelphia until June 1778. Then, they moved onto New York.

OLD PINE STREET ⬢4 PRESBYTERIAN CHURCH AND HISTORIC GRAVEYARD

412 PINE STREET
OPEN MONDAY – FRIDAY, 10 – 3
TOURS BY RESERVATION ONLY   FREE ADMISSION

Exit Washington Square Park at 6th Street, and walk toward the intersection of 6th and Walnut Streets, but do not cross Walnut. Make a right and continue on 6th Street, passing Locust and Spruce Streets. When you reach the intersection of 6th and Pine Streets, turn left onto Pine, walking in the direction of 4th Street. Old Pine Street Presbyterian Church is before the intersection of 4th and Pine Streets.

The "Church of the Patriots," as it was once called, stands on its original foundation and retains its original brick walls from 1768. Burials in the graveyard began as early as May 1768—fifty Revolutionary War soldiers are buried here in the graveyard.

When the British marched through Philadelphia, they converted the church to a hospital, using the pews and pulpit for firewood to keep their soldiers warm. As an additional insult to the Patriots and parishioners, 100 Hessian mercenaries were buried in the graveyard, next to the American soldiers. Mysteriously, those 100 Hessians were moved to a mass grave at some point outside the graveyard.

They say many a Founding Father haunt this graveyard. Disembodied voices and noises are heard at night. I can only imagine who or what type of energy survived from the British occupation days. With the strength of emotion from military occupation coupled with the destruction of a House of God at the hands of the British Army, I am sure many a soul have returned to protest the actions of the British and to protect the church.

⑤ ST. PETER'S CHURCH
AND GRAVEYARD

PINE STREET BETWEEN 3RD AND 4TH STREETS
OPEN MONDAY – FRIDAY, 8:30 – 4
SATURDAY 8:30 – 3   FREE ADMISSION

As you exit Pine Street Presbyterian Church and Graveyard, turn right and continue to travel on Pine Street toward 3rd Street (in the same direction). St. Peter's Church is between 3rd and 4th Streets on the right side of Pine Street.
    Robert Smith, the man who built Carpenter's Hall, also raised St. Peter's, which opened in 1761 to accommodate the overcrowded Christ Church. George Washington and Mayor Samuel Powel worshipped here, and sat in pew 41. Seven Native American chiefs, as well as naval hero Stephen Decatur, are buried here in the graveyard.
    The graveyard at St. Peter's is the site of reports of a phantom woman who appears every night around nine o'clock. Popular belief is that she is some type of protector of the souls buried here. The chiefs are active in the graveyard, too, and have been witnessed moving around in what has been described as a restless manner. Sightings of the ghost of Stephen Decatur have also been reported.
    Finally, there have also been sightings of an "unknown" ghost. The first sightings date back to the year 1834. Identity and gender are unknown and indistinguishable. The ghost always walks in the same pattern through the graveyard. He or she meanders between the rows of worn out tombstones, never acknowledging the living or anyone else. Then, the ghost vanishes into thin air close to the church yard wall. Its movements are stiff, rigid, and very quiet.
    Other sightings include a phantom horse-drawn carriage speeding through the graveyard. In *Annals of Philadelphia*, Mr. Watson describes a phantom carriage charging through the city:

> Seeing a black coach driven about at midnight by an evil spirit, having there in one of our deceased rich citizens, who was deemed to have died with unkind feelings to one dependent upon him... there were people enough who were quite persuaded that they saw it! This was before the Revolution.

I am unsure if these two phantom carriage stories are related. However, they are the only two ghost carriages I have found in my research. Two things about Watson's account of the phantom carriage I find particularly fascinating:

First is the colonial concept of the duty of the wealthy to be charitable to those less fortunate in society. This concept is to be expected especially if those less fortunate are relatives. Compassion and duty are second nature in Colonial society. Ignoring one's duty and being unkind and uncharitable is considered unacceptable. It is also punishable in the afterlife. Second is the punishment itself. The bad rich man is now damned to ride in an unholy, terrifying carriage driven by an evil spirit. It is most ironic to punish him with a device of servitude. This uncompassionate wealthy man most likely had his own carriage and driver, both of which he probably abused, and he is now condemned to ride in what was once a symbol of his wealth with a demonic driver. It seems like a warning of what will happen to you if you are neither a charitable person nor kind to your fellow man. It also makes me wonder how many filthy rich dead people are condemned to ride in limousines driven by demons. It is definitely Karma served on an 18th-century platter—food for thought.

As you stroll down the road, beware of the Hag of Pine Street. This entity was a grumpy old woman in life and has not changed her demeanor in death. She screams at kids at play, harasses young affectionate couples and yells at anyone who plays the piano too loudly.

St. Peter's Graveyard in Society Hill.

Laurel Hill Cemetery.

Holy Redeemer Cemetery in Bridesburg.

24

THE PHYSICK HOUSE 6

321 SOUTH 4TH STREET
OPEN THURSDAY – SATURDAY, 12 – 5   THERE IS AN ADMISSION FEE
SUNDAY, 1 – 5   FOR THIS STOP

Exit St. Peter's Church and Graveyard, turn left, and walk on Pine Street toward the intersection at 4th Street. Turn right onto 4th Street, crossing Pine Street, and travel north in the direction of Spruce Street. The Physick House is on the right side of 4th Street before the intersection at Spruce Street.

Philip Syng Physick owned this house, which was built in 1786. Often called the "Father of American Surgery," he performed operations in the days before anesthesia.

In the 1790s, Physick and his wife were in the middle of a rather unpleasant divorce. Divorce itself was highly unusual during the Colonial Era. It was not unusual, however, for couples to separate, with one spouse moving to another colony, such as the Massachusetts Bay Colony or Virginia. Judging by Mrs. Physick's appearance, no one would guess the disagreeable nature of the divorce or the stress she suffered. One could even say she was of a tranquil disposition. But *tranquilized* would be a better word for it, because, apparently, the Father of American Surgery regularly sedated his wife with opium. She was left in a euphoric, or, relaxed, state, to wander the house and the backyard, where she would sit under her favorite tree in peace.

It is believed that Physick, himself, haunts his house—possibly out of guilt or remorse. However, sightings of his wife began when the tree was cut down and removed from the property. This is not surprising: spiritual activity is often the result of renovations or demolition. Her ghost is described as resembling a beautiful woman wearing a lavender gown and sobbing.

SUPERNATURAL DATA: residual haunting

In a residual haunting, the spirit or ghost follows his or her own agenda and rarely acknowledges the living witnesses. The ghost is trapped in a haunted revival, or play, of a certain (traumatic) event, and is forced to relive it over and over again. The event itself is the focal point—not the ghostly players. In most cases, they are robotic in their repetition of events.

7 THE POWEL HOUSE

244 SOUTH 3RD STREET
OPEN THURSDAY – SATURDAY 12 – 5   THERE IS AN ADMISSION FEE
SUNDAY, 1– 5   FOR THIS STOP

As you exit the Physick House, turn right and walk along 4th Street in the direction of Spruce Street. At the intersection, turn right on Spruce Street. Walk east and turn left onto 3rd. The Powel House is on the left side of 3rd Street.

Samuel Powel, the last mayor of Philadelphia under British rule and the first of the new republic, purchased the house in 1769. Mrs. Powel hosted many lavish parties here, and welcomed many distinguished guests: John Adams, Benjamin Franklin, the Marquis de Lafayette, and even Benedict Arnold and his wife Peggy Shippen. Mayor Powel died in 1790, a victim of the Yellow Fever Epidemic.

This house is one of the most spiritually active in the city. Edwin Moore saw the ghost of the Marquis de Lafayette and apparitions of several Continental Army officers. Infamous traitor, Benedict Arnold has been sighted here, as well. The rumor is that he has unfinished business.

In 1965, historian Edwin Moore and his wife hosted an authentic 18th-century ball here. While searching for an authentic period costume to wear, Mrs. Moore bought a beige and lavender colored gown she thought was perfect for the occasion. There have been sightings since then of a lovely young woman dressed in the same beige and lavender gown Mrs. Moore eventually wore to the 18th-century-themed ball. She fans herself in the second floor drawing room. When discovered by the living, she smiles and then vanishes. She is Peggy Shippen, wife of Benedict Arnold and known Loyalist sympathizer. Peggy Shippen wore that same gown to the last ball she attended at the Powel House. Perhaps she is temporarily returning to a happier time and location.

SUPERNATURAL DATA: ectoplasm

Ectoplasm is believed to be the byproduct of a manifestation of spiritual energy.

THE BISHOP WHITE HOUSE ⑧

309 Walnut Street
Open Wednesday – Sunday

*See Independence Visitor's Center
for free tour and tickets*

As you leave the Powel House, turn left and continue walking in the same direction on 3rd Street to Walnut Street, and cross Walnut. The Bishop White House is close to the intersection of 3rd and Walnut Streets, on the left side of Walnut.

Bishop William White was Rector of both Christ Church and St. Peter's Church, and the first Episcopal Bishop in the Commonwealth of Pennsylvania. From 1777 to 1789, he was the Chaplain to the First Continental Congress. He is buried under the altar at Christ Church. Many of the Founding Fathers visited the Bishop and his family, including George Washington and Benjamin Franklin.

The Bishop White House is often referred to as a very "spooky place" and sometimes a very "creepy place," too. The park rangers have reported feeling uneasy here when guiding tours, especially in the kitchen area. I have also heard that they avoid entering the house alone or in the evening. One of the National Park Service archive librarians strongly advised me to take the tour of the house and try to see the basement. Rumor has it, the further you walk into the house, the more uneasy you feel; the deeper you travel into the house the more haunted it is—so they say. There is definitely a very strong energy surrounding this house. As you make your way through into the kitchen, you can feel the energy vortex growing stronger and stronger. I can only imagine the intensity of the energy in the basement. You absolutely want to make sure you do proper grounding after a visit here.

Mrs. Boggs was the Bishop's maid in 1790. It is believed to be her ghost that has appeared to people on the Philly Ghost tour. Visitors and tourists have also reported sightings of a phantom cat in the window. However, no cat lives here now, nor did the Bishop own a cat.

THE TODD HOUSE

4th and Walnut Streets
Hours: same as the Bishop White House
A tour of the Todd House is included on the ticket for the tour of The Bishop White House

27

Lawyer John Todd lived here with his famous wife, Dolley. In the midst of the Yellow Fever Epidemic, John Todd sent Dolley and their month-old son Thomas to the country to save them from becoming victims of the epidemic. Mr. Todd remained in the city to tend to the legal needs of the afflicted. Unfortunately, Dolley's husband and son both succumbed to yellow fever. She later married James Madison and became the First Lady when her husband was elected the fourth President of the United States.

Dolley's ghost seems to avoid the City of Brotherly Love, opting to haunt Washington, D.C., where she spent her time as First Lady and many happy years afterwards. If there is any supernatural activity in the Todd House, it is as of yet undetected. Perhaps John Todd will return to his home someday. Perhaps you will be the one to capture his apparition on film—anything is possible!

Historical Data:
The Yellow Fever Epidemic of 1793

In 1793, the population of the City of Philadelphia was 55,000. It was the Capital City of the new country, the largest city in America, and had the busiest port. The summer of 1793 proved to be extremely hot and dry. The water levels in the wells and streams were dangerously low. This was an ideal breeding situation for insects, and July saw a huge increase in the number of flies, and, especially, mosquitoes. The influx of political refugees from the Caribbean also increased. It was these refugees who initially brought the Yellow Fever into the city, and the growing mosquito population that spread it. Mosquitoes basically did their job, first biting an infected person and then biting a healthy person, thus infecting that healthy person. Symptoms of the disease included pains in the back, head, and limbs and a high fever. The symptoms would disappear and then reappear with a vengeance. Death soon followed. The medical community was baffled. Dr. Benjamin Rush worked day and night to fight the disease and save lives. Unfortunately, Colonial medicine was primitive at best and served as no credible threat whatsoever to the monster that was Yellow Fever. President George Washington, his cabinet, and Congress fled the city. The disease began to disappear as the cold weather arrived in the city, but not before it took 2000 victims.

BENJAMIN RUSH HOUSE 9
AND 18TH CENTURY GARDEN

Very near the Bishop White House and the 18th Century Garden, Benjamin Rush's house once stood. Dr. Benjamin Rush was one of the most influential physicians and public health figures in the colonies, and his clinical analysis set standards for American medicine. He was also the first United States Surgeon General and became Treasurer of the United States Mint in 1799. An evergreen and holly garden stands on the site of his house. It is a true 18th-century-style garden, inside of which are a few benches.

Dr. Rush's ghost has been seen walking around where his house used to stand. Oh, the phantom cat: the one in the window of the Bishop White House. There is a very good possibility it is Dr. Rush's cat, lounging in his neighbor's window.

PHILADELPHIA MERCHANTS' 10
EXCHANGE BUILDING

3RD AND WALNUT STREETS
THE LOBBY IS OPEN TO THE PUBLIC
THE LIBRARY AND ARCHIVES IS OPEN FOR RESEARCH BY APPOINTMENT

The Philadelphia Merchants' Exchange building is across 3rd Street, less than a block east of the Bishop White House, on the same side of Walnut Street.

Philadelphia architect William Strickland designed this building, which served as both a stock exchange and place where merchants could meet to trade their goods, in 1832. Now it houses the regional offices of the National Park Service, and only the lobby is open to the public. The Library and Archives, which is not only impressive, but truly inspiring, is on the third floor.

The inside of the Merchants' Exchange Building is not haunted, but there is some interesting energy in the library. I think the various scattered energies are the result of the age of the materials in the archives, and, because the room is much smaller than a public library, for instance, the energy is much more concentrated, yet very interesting and positive. The same cannot be said for the area directly in front of the building. It is definitely haunted, for there is evidence of a residual haunting occurring there. Some people call it Osteen's Revenge; others call it Osteen's Poetic Justice. Whatever it is, it is most certainly karmic and a product of the universe's magic.

In the 19th century, Jack Osteen, a blind vagrant, or, beggar, was very well known in the area surrounding 3rd and Walnut Streets. People and animals alike felt an affinity for Jack, who was kind and endearing. One horse in particular took a very strong liking to Jack, as Jack would pet him and give him

treats, like apples. The owner of the horse (and carriage) was a very wealthy businessman named Harold Thorn. In terms of personality, he and Jack were polar opposites.

Harold Thorn was not compassionate, and, as a result, no friend to animals, especially his own horse. One day, Thorn suffered a huge financial defeat that left him enraged. Shortly afterwards, he encountered Jack Osteen. Unfortunately, the blind man walked into Thorn and stepped on his foot. Thorn went into a fit and beat Jack Osteen to death with his walking stick. He passed on all of his rage and anger to the poor blind beggar.

After he killed Jack Osteen, Thorn's horse (and Osteen's friend) reacted. He reared up, let out a vengeful neigh, and kicked his owner to death.

To this day, just before dawn, a shadow figure appears in front of the Merchants' Exchange Building. The shadow man disappears quickly, about the same time phantom hoof beats are heard.

Animals are believed to be sensitive to supernatural energy or activity. This may explain why, occasionally, they seem to chase, play with, and stare intensely and bark at absolutely nothing.

THE CITY TAVERN 11

138 SOUTH 2ND STREET
OPEN DAILY AT 11AM

You can see the back porch of the City Tavern from The Merchants' Exchange Courtyard, and there is a paved path lined with flower pots behind the Merchants Exchange Building that leads from the courtyard to the back of the City Tavern.

The City Tavern was the place to be in the country's early days. It was not only a place to eat a fine meal and drink a few pints; it was also the Patriot's political epicenter, where you could engage in after-dinner conversation about liberty with colonial bigwigs like George Washington, Benjamin Franklin, and Thomas Jefferson. The building on the corner of Second and Walnut Streets is a recreation of the original structure, which stood on the same spot. In the mid 1800s, a fire destroyed the original City Tavern. It was reconstructed in 1975, but this particularly destructive fire gave the Tavern its most famous ghost—a bride who died in the blaze during her wedding party.

Many patrons have held formal events and celebrations here over the years, including weddings, and cameras have reportedly captured the bride's ghostly image on numerous occasions. The results range from double exposures to an actual transparent woman. Of course, no one ever remembers seeing her at the party; she only appears on film. Other accounts tell of a female figure, a lady in white wandering around on the upper floors. In one documented case, a young woman who was attending a function at the City Tavern dropped her camera when she felt a sharp, burning sensation on her hand. Oddly enough, there were no candles, matches, or anything else that would produce fire in close proximity to the woman.

I have my own story about the City Tavern. My friend Brian Kelly and I were taking pictures for this book. It was an unseasonably warm November afternoon. I took a few pictures of the City Tavern sign, then we moved to the back of the restaurant. As previously mentioned, there is a courtyard behind the restaurant with an attached porch. Brian took pictures with his digital camera that were hazy and dull, appearing almost whitewashed. This was not a camera malfunction, however: all of the pictures he took before and after this were clear and crisp, and the camera battery was fully charged. The camera strangeness does not end here.

The photos I took of the City Tavern sign, the courtyard, and view of the back of the Merchants' Exchange building were all fine. We decided to test this again. About a week later, we were in Society Hill, so we took a different route to the City Tavern. The photos he took of the rear of the restaurant and courtyard were taken from the corner facing the Merchants' Exchange Building. Again, all of Brian's pictures had a hazy, worn out look to them. Again, my photos were clear. So, whatever spirits are lurking in the restaurant and courtyard have no problem with my photographs. They apparently do not want Brian to take any pictures whatsoever.

Historical Data: The Delaware River

Not only did the Delaware River provide the colonists a port through which daily necessities, goods, and supplies arrived from other countries, and give sailors and merchants their livelihood, but it was also a source of well deserved entertainment for the hard working citizens of Philadelphia. In the 18th and 19th Centuries, the river froze in the harsh winter months, giving Philadelphians a natural ice skating rink.

Mr. Watson describes this unusual activity in *Annals of Philadelphia*:

"On days the Delaware was frozen, booths were put up to sell refreshments to the gathered crowd; sometimes an ox roast would add to the excitement. Horses were also specially shod for racing sleighs on the solid river and the course would go miles upstream. The ice could get so thick…that horses pulled loaded ferryboats across the channel atop the ice."

WATER STREET 12

As you exit the City Tavern, turn left onto 2nd Street toward the intersection of 2nd and Chestnut Streets. Cross and turn right onto Chestnut Street. Begin walking on Chestnut Street toward the intersection of Chestnut and Front Streets. Turn left on Front Street and walk toward Market Street. If Water Street still existed, it would probably be located somewhere along Interstate 95. If you walk through the Philadelphia Parking Authority Lot on Front Street and look through the fencing to the highway beneath, that would be Water Street.

However, in the early days of the city (and country), it was bustling with the activity of waterfront taverns and very colorful characters. Residents of the growing port city of Philadelphia had a plethora of drinking establishments to choose from on Water Street. Some of the tavern names on the infamous pirates' hangout included "The Battle of the Kegs," "Cork Arms," "Ship," and "Three Jolly Irishmen" (colorful names for colorful institutions that served very colorful patrons). Interstate 95 transformed Front Street, and Water and Noble Streets were two of its victims.

Water Street was notorious for pirate activity and some other types of unsavory characters, as well. A popular docking space for ships was the area between Walnut and Dock Streets, near Water Street. The Blue Anchor Tavern was built near Walnut Street due to its proximity to the docks. Rumor has it that a man named Edward Teach, (a.k.a. Blackbeard), and William "Captain" Kidd patronized the Blue Anchor Tavern, where William Penn, ironically, was also a patron. Pirates' preference for Philadelphia was directly related to the leniency of the Quaker justice and prison system at that time, which would not remain that way for long. There are also stories of pirate treasure buried along the waterfront.

Water Street may not be the same, physically, as in the days of the early colonies, but it is still a favorite spot of pirate ghosts. The imposing pirate ghosts appear on Front Street, in between Walnut and Chestnut Streets. Not surprisingly, the pirate apparitions like to show themselves very late at night to unsuspecting pedestrians. Perhaps they are still looking for victims to Shanghai onto their pirate ships. Remember the infamous pirate Wilkinson who was hanged at the Walnut Street Prison? His ghost is just one of the pirates who swagger down Water Street looking for mischief. Blackbeard and Captain Kidd may also be returning to their old stomping grounds. Perhaps they are looking for buried treasure, or for a ghostly version of the Blue Anchor Tavern or one of the other long gone drinking establishments of the 18th century?

Mr. Watson, in *Annals of Philadelphia*, names two haunted houses in the waterfront area, both located on Second Street:

"Emlen's house, at the southwest corner of Noble and Second Streets; Naglee's house, far out Second Street. Near the rope walk—there was a man to be seen hanging without a head."

13 ELFRETH'S ALLEY AND MUSEUM

126 ELFRETH'S ALLEY
OFF 2ND STREET, BETWEEN RACE AND ARCH STREETS
OPEN TUESDAY – SATURDAY, 10 – 5
THERE IS AN ADMISSION FEE FOR THE MUSEUM

Please remember that the houses in Elfreth's Alley and Bladen's Court are private residences, so be respectful when taking pictures, etc.

From the intersection of Front and Chestnut Streets, continue walking on Front Street, heading in the direction of Market Street. Turn left on Market at the statue of Chief Tamanend. There is also a Septa bus terminal there. Walk to 2nd Street via Market Street, but do not cross the intersection. Turn right, remain on 2nd Street and travel toward Arch Street. Cross Arch Street. Elfreth's Alley is just a few feet from the intersection of 2nd and Arch Streets. It is on the right side of 2nd.

The Elfreth's Alley Museum is No. 126 on the street. It is our nation's oldest continuous residential street. Once occupied by the colonial working class, Elfreth's Alley has become one of the most visited streets in the city of Philadelphia. As you stroll down the cobblestone alley, you are able to get an idea of what colonial Philadelphia looked like. Maybe you will see something mysterious and supernatural, too! No. 120 and No. 122 are the oldest homes, built between 1724 and 1728. No 126 was built by Jeremiah Elfreth in 1755. Now, it is the Elfreth's Alley Museum. Bladen's Court consists of three houses and a courtyard and is tucked neatly behind Elfreth's Alley. This is truly one of the most quaint, picturesque places in the City of Philadelphia.

A shy, reliable source shared this tale of a sighting of a ghost during my last visit to the museum. During the World War I era, the ghost of a woman in a long white nightgown was seen moving back and forth between the rooms of No. 126. She had very long dark hair (almost black), which she was brushing, and was also described as gliding, not stepping or walking, from room to room, unaware of the living person(s) in the room.

Historical Data:
The Role of Women in Colonial Philadelphia

Women (and children) were seen but not heard, especially in public, in Colonial Philadelphia. That is to say, women were not viewed as citizens with the same rights and liberties as men, and they had no political rights. They were publicly represented by the heads of their respective households, also known as their husbands (and fathers). Most likely this was because women were incapable of being in public without adult male supervision. As a male dominated society, this was very typical.

Only the wealthiest families educated their daughters formally. That was an honor and a privilege usually reserved for boys. The role of the housewife was far more rigorous and physically challenging in the days of early America than it is today. Being a housewife meant being a clothes designer and tailor, family physician, accountant, butcher as well as cook, teacher, and housekeeper, to name just a few roles.

Aside from being the family caretakers, women had no careers or professions during the Colonial Era. If a woman was in business or had a career, it was because she was a widow and the male heir(s) were too young to undertake a profession. Then and only then was a woman trusted with a career. This double standard was as close as society had come to equality.

Wives were expected to provide assistance to their husbands in every possible way and serve in silence. When their husbands joined the Continental Army and went off to war with General Washington, the women of the home front assumed all the responsibilities. They became surrogate shopkeepers, shoemakers, blacksmiths, candle makers, and farmers: Colonial precursors to Rosie the Riveter. However, they did this in addition to their regular duties, like making butter and cheese, spinning wool, making and mending all clothing, tending to the herb and vegetable garden(s), milking cows, raising the children, being the family physician, and let's not forget, butchering the meat, when needed. More than likely, they did all this while nursing a baby.

Lastly, women married young and began having babies almost immediately. A woman during the Colonial Era gave birth to six, eight, or more children. Not all babies lived to adult- or even childhood. Betsy Ross, for example, had six babies, but only four lived. It was not unusual for both mothers and their older daughters to be pregnant at the same time. Life in the colonies was hard and demanding, and only the strong survived.

BETSY ROSS HOUSE (14)

239 ARCH STREET   THERE IS AN ADMISSION FEE FOR THIS STOP
OPEN DAILY, 10 – 5   AUDIO GUIDES ARE AVAILABLE

As you exit Elfreth's Alley, turn left onto 2nd Street, travel in the direction of Arch Street, and turn right onto Arch. Betsy Ross House is in the middle of the block on the right side of Arch Street.

Her Georgian style house, built around 1740, is known as the "Birthplace of Old Glory." Well known for her embroidery skills, Betsy Ross ran an upholstery and flag-making business and sewed pennants and insignia for the state navy. In May 1776, George Washington, Robert Morris, and George Ross, Betsy's husband's uncle and a delegate to the Continental Congress, asked her to design a flag. Her invention—alternating red and white stripes and 13 five-pointed stars on a blue field—was adopted by the Continental Congress on June 14, 1777.

Betsy Ross was an extraordinary woman. She lived to be 84 years old, outliving three husbands and giving birth to a total of seven children. Elizabeth Griscom Ross Ashbourne Claypoole was her full name. While visiting her house,

I discovered new information about Mrs. Ross and the role she played in the colonies' struggle for liberty and independence, as, recently, historical archivists have uncovered previously unknown facts regarding her life as a patriot.

Apparently, Mrs. Ross was not a sweet, delicate woman wearing a white cap and sewing quietly in a corner by candle light. We were spoon fed that image from our grade school social studies classes and history programs as children. As a matter of fact, she was not submissive or passive at all.

Her participation in the revolution was not only active, but quite dangerous. She worked at night by candle light, making musket balls in the basement of her house. Imminent danger from working with explosives was not the only life threatening aspect of this activity: making musket balls for the Continental Army was viewed as an act of treason by the British government. Mrs. Ross was not a soldier. She was a woman, obviously, and, as 18th-century views of women were quite primitive and unforgiving, her punishment would have been very severe and final (immediate execution). Plus, the British may have extracted "justice" from her family members. Other new information recovered has also revealed she lived in this particular house from 1776 to 1779. Her husband, John was in his twenties when he died in this house.

The house itself has seen its owners change throughout the years. It even went into a period when its future was unknown before becoming a national treasure. Charles Weiserberger bought the house in 1898 and opened the first floor to the public as a museum. He was a very generous man, who believed in the preservation and sharing of history. Unfortunately, he died while preparing for his daughter's birthday celebration. It is believed he never really left the house.

This house is very active with both feminine human energy and spirit energy. The women, like Mrs. Ross, who work, volunteer, and keep this place running on a daily basis, are extraordinary. You can feel that energy of devotion when you visit this house. Betsy Ross's ghost has been sighted at the foot of her bed, crying. Her spectral voice is heard in the basement saying, "Pardon me." Mrs. Ross' ghostly image has also been reported in the vicinity of her final resting place.

Rachel Costa portrays Betsy Ross in the house and shared some experiences with me. She has witnessed various alarms being set off at different times in the duration of a day with no apparent reason. In one instance, Rachel went into Betsy's workshop where the alarm was sounding and she noticed one of the spools of thread had been moved from its designated place. These are not the same thread spools as the ones in your mom's sewing kit. They are about six inches in height and two inches in diameter, requiring two hands to move one. Another staff member, Sandy, experienced a grey, fog-like mist gliding across the room in which she was working. This was late in the afternoon, near sunset, on a dry autumn day. That does not match fog inducing conditions, like humidity or early morning hours.

BETSY ROSS

ELIZABETH GRISCOM CLAYPOOLE
JANUARY 1, 1752 — JANUARY 30, 1836
AND HER HUSBAND
JOHN CLAYPOOLE
AUGUST 15, 1752 — AUGUST 3, 1817

In my own experience, I have felt two distinctive types of energy in the upstairs level of the house. Both were positive sources of energy, and one was definitely feminine. Hopefully, it was Mrs. Ross watching over us. The other presence was neither feminine nor nurturing. However, it was very peaceful, content and at home in the house. I was extremely lucky to capture one of the entities on film. What I should say is, I was extremely fortunate one of the entities allowed herself to be photographed! It is definitely a female spirit on the staircase leading from Betsy's bedroom to her workshop. We were in the workshop when two tourists (a mother and daughter) from New Zealand came in for photos with Betsy. I moved so they could be photographed together and snapped the picture of the staircase. I never thought I would be lucky enough to get this photo! Many gracious thanks to Mrs. Ross. Needless to say, I take pictures of all staircases in all locations now.

CHRIST CHURCH 15
BURIAL GROUND

5TH AND ARCH STREETS
OPEN MONDAY – SATURDAY, 10 – 4
SUNDAY, 12 – 4
WEATHER PERMITTING

THERE IS AN ADMISSION FEE
FOR THIS STOP

As you exit the Betsy Ross House, turn right and continue walking on Arch Street toward 5th Street. The exact location of Christ Church Burial Ground is in the middle of the block on Arch Street. You will see the Burial Ground entrance before the intersection of 5th and Arch Streets. The grave of Benjamin Franklin can be viewed through the iron bars directly on the southeast corner of 5th and Arch Streets. Christ Church is located on Second Street, between Arch and Market Streets.

As a group, the Continental Congress attended religious services at Christ Church in 1775. The famous colonial parishioners who worshipped here include: George Washington, Benjamin Franklin, Robert Morris, and Betsy Ross.

"Show me your cemeteries and I will tell you what kind of people you have."

– Benjamin Franklin

The Christ Church Burial Ground is the final resting place of many notable Philadelphians: Benjamin Franklin, and four signers of the Declaration of Independence—Dr. Benjamin Rush, Francis Hopkinson, George Ross, and Joseph Hewes. Betsy Ross's remains were moved here after her initial burial at Mount Moriah Cemetery in southwest Philadelphia. Mr. Franklin's grave can be seen from the sidewalk through the black iron railing. It has become a tradition to leave a penny behind on Mr. Franklin's grave, and a caretaker sweeps all the pennies off Mr. Franklin's grave several times a day.

Mr. Franklin's spirit seems to take his quote, "A penny saved is a penny earned," quite literally. One night, in 1976, close to 8pm or so, a nurse from one of the area hospitals was waiting for a bus right next to the burial ground, just a few feet from Mr. Franklin's grave. She heard the "ping" noise coins make when they hit the sidewalk, then turned to find herself alone. A minute later, the same thing happened. Again, she saw no one. It happened a third time. By now, she was quite angry. She spun around to give the kids whom she thought had been throwing the pennies a verbal lashing. However, she only saw Mr. Franklin's grave, and with that a strange feeling grew in her stomach. Perhaps our Founding Father was making a statement of his own?

In 1728, when he was just 23 years old, Benjamin Franklin wrote his own epitaph. While it is dry and humorous, it is also a little sad and morbid, too:

The Body of
B. Franklin, Printer,
(Like the Cover of an Old Book
Its Contents Torn Out
And Stript of its Lettering and Gilding)
Lies Here, Food for Worms,
But the Work Shall Not be Lost
For it will (as He Believ'd) Appear Once More
In a New and More Elegant Edition
Revised and Corrected
By the Author

SECOND BANK 16
OF THE UNITED STATES

420 Chestnut Street
Open Wednesday – Sunday, 11 – 5

As you exit Christ Church Burial Ground, turn left, remain on 5th Street and walk toward Arch Street. Turn left on 5th Street and walk in the direction of Chestnut Street. Cross Market Street, remaining on 5th Street. When you reach the intersection of 5th and Chestnut Streets, turn left onto Chestnut. The Second Bank of the U.S. is in between 5th and 4th Streets on Chestnut Street, on the right side of the street.

The Second Bank of the United States is the large, elegant Parthenon look-alike, built in 1834. It is the home of many portraits of our Founding Fathers, which include, but are not limited to, George Washington, Thomas Jefferson, and the Marquis de Lafayette. It is also the location of a very intriguing event.

The following paranormal event is one of the strangest I have uncovered in my research—very strange and very mysterious. The story begins in England. From 1850 to 1904, women were randomly attacked in streets. The culprit was a monster, an animal like entity that was given the name Spring Heel'd Jack. The creature had claws instead of hands and shot flames from its mouth. Unsuspecting women were grabbed and dragged into alleyways, where the monster clawed at their throats and faces.

In May 1905, Julia McGlone was the housekeeper/cleaner at the Second Bank of the United States. She had completed her duties and was leaving the bank from a side exit door, which led to the alley. Someone or something grabbed her from the shadows. It was ripping and clawing the flesh on her neck and face. A police officer intervened and tried to rescue her, but the entity threw him across the alley like he was a child's toy. When questioned by more police officers, they both gave the same description: it was wearing a weird helmet; its eyes were red like fire; blue flames shot from its mouth; it had no hands, but instead, it had claws; and its skin was tight and thick and felt as if it had been oiled. This was the same description given of England's Spring Heel'd Jack. Perhaps Jack relocated from England to America? If so, it must have taken him almost a full year to travel across the ocean!

17 THE FIRST BANK
OF THE UNITED STATES

3RD AND CHESTNUT STREETS

This site is usually closed to the public. However, contact the National Park Service to see if a special tour is available.

As you exit the Second Bank of the U.S., turn right on Chestnut Street and walk toward 3rd Street, crossing 4th Street. Turn right on 3rd Street. The First Bank of the U.S. is only a few feet away.

The First Bank of the United States is barely a block from the Second Bank of the United States. It is the oldest bank building in the country. The bank operations began in Carpenter's Hall, and were then moved to 3rd and Chestnut Streets after completion of the building. It was the government's bank headquarters from 1799 to 1811.

Alexander Hamilton was Treasury Secretary from 1789 to 1795. In 1804, he had his famous and fatal duel with Aaron Burr. Days after the duel, Mr. Hamilton's ghost was sighted in the bank. In 1811, the First Bank was purchased by Stephen Girard, who brought in a Catholic priest to exorcise the building. Sightings of Hamilton's ghost have become less and less frequent, but never completely ceased.

18 CARPENTER'S HALL

325 CHESTNUT STREET
OPEN WEDNESDAY – SUNDAY 10 – 4   FREE ADMISSION

Carpenter's Hall is tucked behind the Signer's Garden, between the First Bank of the U.S. and 3rd Street, between Chestnut and Walnut Streets.

The Carpenter's Company, founded in 1724, is the oldest builder's organization in the United States. It was the site of many significant events, which include serving as a meeting place for the First Continental Congress in 1774 and housing the offices of the Secretary of War in 1790 and 1791. The offices and vaults of the First Bank of the United States were here from 1791 to 1797. It is the oldest existing trade guild in the United States. Part of Benjamin Franklin's library is on the second floor.

Carpenter's Hall is haunted by some of its former residents. The supernatural events here have been and continue to be very active and unusual. The attic was divided into apartments during its early years and rented to members of the Carpenter's Company—to unmarried members, in particular, because the rooms were so tiny.

In 1789, one of its members was implicated in a bank robbery. Two men robbed the vault in the basement for more than $160,000. Can you imagine how much money that would translate into today? The police arrived too late. However, a key left behind led them to two of the members of the company. Tom Cunningham died within a week of moving into one of the apartments in the attic of yellow fever. After his death, all sorts of ghostly noises began: stomping in the hallway and on staircases, and loud, unidentifiable noises coming from his apartment. These sounds continued for decades after rooms were no longer rented to members. In 1857, the building was opened to the public, and the ghostly noises resumed.

In 1960, the Philadelphia Police Department investigated the noises but found no evidence of their origin. There was also an odor—a foul, rotten stench—that seemed to accompany the loud noises. It disappeared the following day. Then, the cycle would repeat itself every few days: noises and a rotten, foul stench at night, gone the next day. This vicious cycle would repeat and continue for years.

In 1974, the city celebrated the Bicentennial Year of the First Continental Congress. Milton Schapp, the governor of Pennsylvania at that time, hosted a meeting of the National Governor's Conference in Carpenter's Hall. The ghosts held back nothing: there was shouting, chairs moving and dragging, disembodied voices, loud arguing. The following morning, the smell of fresh tobacco (not a foul odor) was in the building. It seemed as if the members of the First Continental Congress wanted to join in on the Bicentennial festivities. Maybe they were reliving their glory days? Maybe they will reveal something for the Tercentennial celebration (2074)?

Carpenter's Hall, like Independence Hall, is a structure full of emotional energy. The high energy of rebellion and revolution can be felt as soon as you enter the building: it is brimming with residual energy. Our Founding Fathers were so argumentative, passionate, and full of fury for Liberty. Energy like that does not quietly disappear into the night. Instead, it remains, and this building, like Independence Hall, "shines."

19 LIBRARY HALL

105 SOUTH 5TH STREET
OPEN FOR USE BY SCHOLARS

As you exit Carpenter's Hall, turn right onto 4th Street, walking in the direction of Walnut Street. Turn right onto Walnut at the intersection, traveling toward 5th Street. Turn right onto 5th. Library Hall is directly across 5th Street from the American Philosophical Society, in the middle of the block. You can view the outside of the building from the grounds of Independence Hall, and you can see the grounds of Independence Hall from the front of the Library Hall Building.

The structure that stands on 5th Street, the oldest subscription library in the United States, is a 20th-century reconstruction of Benjamin Franklin's Library Company of Philadelphia. It now houses the Library of the American Philosophical Society, also founded by Mr. Franklin, in 1743. It contains his books and papers along with the original journals of the Lewis and Clark Expedition and a copy of the Declaration of Independence in Thomas Jefferson's handwriting. Famous historical members include George Washington, Thomas Jefferson, Thomas Paine, Alexander Hamilton, John Adams, and the Marquis de Lafayette. They could read documents, books, and more at the library, or borrow books. The statue of Benjamin Franklin atop the door to Library Hall is quite unusual. He is dressed in a toga, traditional ancient Greek and Roman attire, not the traditional Colonial male attire.

Benjamin Franklin's ghost is a regular patron here. A cleaning woman reported seeing his ghost as a cheerful man dressed in 18th-century fashion. She saw his ghost on a regular basis (almost daily) as she did her morning cleaning. Mr. Franklin carried books from room to room, and, on occasion, climbed the ladder for books on the high shelves. He also talked to himself. Sometimes he paced back and forth or would lean over a table filled with papers with an intense look on his face, deep in thought.

One day, while rushing to go from one room of the library to another, he knocked over the cleaning lady. She lectured him about how a gentleman like him should have better manners. Then, she followed him down the hallway, continuing to give him a verbal lashing. Mr. Franklin's ghost finally turned around, folded his hands and bowed in apology to the irritated cleaning woman. After that event, his ghost began avoiding rooms when the cleaning lady was in them. He would sometimes peek around corners and in doors to see if she was in a particular room. Sometimes, if Mr. Franklin's ghost saw her in the hallway, he would actually turn around and walk away from her to avoid confrontation. Also, the toga-clad statue of Mr. Franklin comes to life and dances around in the middle of 5th Street. This ghostly statue dance is supposed to occur very early in the morning, every Easter Sunday.

TOURIST TIP:

If you truly wish to experience liberty the way the Colonial Philadelphians did, visit these sites in the summer months. It will be very hot, but, then again, it was hot in the City of Brotherly Love in the 18th century, too. In case you are wondering how the raw emotions of rebellion and revolution survived, visit the sites in the dead of summer and try to imagine how George Washington, Benjamin Franklin, Thomas Jefferson, John Adams, Patrick Henry, and all other Patriots not only endured the heat of the summer (no air conditioning in the fancy hotel), but the heated arguments amongst themselves, as well.

Also, they did not wear tank tops and flip flops. No, they survived all of the unforgiving heat with their 18th-century clothing, leather riding boots, ruffled, long sleeved shirts, jackets made of wool, and so on. Can you imagine all of that inside Independence Hall and/or Carpenter's Hall in the high noon heat of 90+ degrees, plus the heat of emotion and not a speck of the modern convenience we call anti-perspirant or deodorant? Not to mention the pure tenacity of the Patriots, who were unyielding in their desire to attain freedom and liberty. There are reports of John Adams telling his wife, Abigail to take their children and hide in the woods upon hearing of an impending invasion by the British soldiers. He did not intend to leave the Constitutional Convention in Philadelphia. Liberty, to John Adams, was worthy of any sacrifice.

When I think of Betsy Ross, closed in her basement (with no ventilation), in the summer heat, making musket balls by candle light for the Continental Army, I am in complete awe of her. That is how the energy of rebellion survived: by pure determination, the very same determination and tenacity that made America what it is today. I also wonder how many of us would be willing to make and endure a sacrifice like that. I suppose that is why there is only one General Washington, Mr. Franklin, Mr. Jefferson and Mrs. Ross. May they continue to inspire many more generations of Americans.

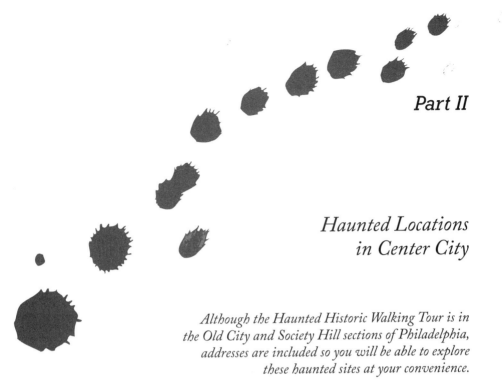

Part II

*Haunted Locations
in Center City*

*Although the Haunted Historic Walking Tour is in
the Old City and Society Hill sections of Philadelphia,
addresses are included so you will be able to explore
these haunted sites at your convenience.*

WALNUT STREET THEATER

825 WALNUT STREET

If you travel down Walnut Street away from Independence Hall to 8th Street, the theater is about two blocks away.

Founded in 1809, this is the oldest English speaking theater in the United States of America. It has staged theatrical performances as well as equine ones, and in 1831–1832, a rhinoceros was even put on the bill here. It is also home to a few ghosts: a litter girl in turn-of-the-century (18th to 19th) clothing has been seen here. An elderly couple, regular patrons when they were alive, returns to their seats as ghosts during performances. There also have been reports of disembodied voices.

Then, there is this outrageous story: It could only happen in the theater! In 1830, John Reed, a.k.a. Pop, was hired as a stage hand. It was his first job and, after many years, he became the theater's doorman. In the forty-four years of his employment, he never missed a performance. He did, however, have a secret, a secret he took to his grave, but not beyond it: his dream to act on stage. He died in 1874 and left very specific, explicit, and peculiar instructions regarding his body and burial thereof. His body was to be separated from his head. His body was to be buried. His head was to be "prepared" and returned to the theater, where it could be the skull of Yorick. Whenever there was a performance of Hamlet in the Walnut Street Theater thereafter, John Reed's skull did in fact portray Yorick. According to theater legend, it vanished.

In 1941, actress Kay Land was appearing in the play "Life with Father". Miss Land decided to do some detective work regarding Pop Reed's skull and located it. Ironically, it was in property storage a few blocks away at the Academy of Music (also haunted). Pop Reed's skull was returned to the Walnut Street Theater in a brown paper bag! Unfortunately, its return was very short lived: it disappeared soon after and remains missing to this day. Only the theater could produce such a dramatic paranormal tale! Hopefully, this tale does not end here. Perhaps some of the unexplained supernatural phenomenon that occur in the Walnut Street Theater is actually John Reed returning to execute his duties there as stage hand, doorman, and Yorick, the King's jester in Hamlet.

Historical Data:
Colonial Medicine

The sources of preventative medicine and practicing medicine in the colonies were basically English/British theory. The colonies were British colonies, and all of the major medical knowledge came from England. Colonial medicine is considered very primitive by today's medical and surgical standards. Treatments sometimes worked, but the attempt often left the patient in a weakened state or dead. The majority of the families during this time treated illnesses themselves. Each family grew an herb garden. Therefore, herbal medicine was widely practiced and easily supplied. Herbs were believed to be able to cure all illnesses. Remedies were very different, as you can see…

There were very few doctors and most were poorly trained; lots of guesswork was involved. In most cases, the cure was much worse than the ailment. Cuts were treated with an ointment made from wild daisies and animal fat. A popular headache cure was sage mixed with animal fat and cornmeal. These mixtures were then applied to the ailing area or ingested. In place of dentists, there were apothecaries. They pulled rotten teeth and sold remedies and herbs.

Many people were bled for more serious ailments. There were two methods: one involved cutting into the infected person's arm to open the vein and let out germs and the "bad" blood; the other involved bleeding by leeches. Obviously, neither method was desirable. These "cures" only made the patient weaker and less equipped to fight illness, which led to death.

Finally, crude medical treatment wouldn't be complete without a crude method of vaccinating patients. Abigail Adams, wife of John, and her children underwent this in order to be vaccinated for small pox. Abigail described this primitive procedure in a letter to him: A needle and thread are drawn through a pox (living germs) on an infected person's arm. That same needle and thread is then drawn through the skin on the arm of a healthy (uninfected) person's arm. This exposed the healthy person to a live virus. Either the person remained healthy and gained immunity from the disease or contracted the disease and possibly died as a result of the vaccination. Needless to say, we have come a long, long way from those early days of Colonial American medicine.

PENNSYLVANIA HOSPITAL

800 SPRUCE STREET

Traveling south on 8th Street to Spruce Street will lead you to Pennsylvania Hospital.

The Pennsylvania Hospital was founded in 1751 by Benjamin Franklin and surgeon Thomas Bond. Its mission was to provide care for the sick, poor, and insane. It is one of the oldest hospitals in the United States, housing the first medical library and the first surgical amphitheater.

The statue of William Penn is also legendary. Mr. Penn's son John donated the statue to the hospital in 1804. Since then, Mr. Penn has overseen the hospital gardens on Pine Street. The ghostly sightings reported on certain evenings—could have been a full moon, could have been New Year's Eve—date back to early in the 19th century. There are many, many versions of this story. In one, the ghost of William Penn's statue is said to step down off his pedestal and walk through the grounds of the hospital. Another version, reported in the Philadelphia Press from 1884, states the ghost of Mr. Penn's statue comes to life when the State House Clock (Independence Hall clock) strikes 6 p.m.

In 1884, nurses from the hospital brought neighborhood children to view William Penn's ghostly statue come to life and walk around. They waited until 6:30 p.m., but Mr. Penn never materialized. The children were disappointed. A few days after this incident, in the early morning hours, Mr. Penn's statue was found face down on the walkway, completely blocking the door to the hospital. While a passing thunderstorm was suspected and blamed, the children believed it was William Penn himself.

BONAPARTE HOUSE

260 South 9th Street

This is a private residence. Please be respectful when taking photographs.

This was once the home of Joseph Bonaparte, ex-King of Spain and Naples, and also the brother of Napoleon Bonaparte. He lived in this house before moving to an estate in Point Breeze on the Delaware River near Bordentown, New Jersey. This private residence has been converted into apartments.

Napoleon's brother does not haunt this house. Joseph Bonaparte haunts another area outside of the city of Philadelphia. We will examine that later, in Chapter Four. The ghost here is a woman named Chloris: her story is one of unrequited love. She fell madly in love with Joseph Bonaparte's steward. The steward, however, was in love and engaged to a Corsican woman, and made plans to journey to Corsica and marry her.

Chloris tried to stow away on the ship, desperately hoping she could change the steward's mind and heart. The ship did not sail, and Chloris was discovered and immediately imprisoned for being a stowaway. Oddly, the prison was located in a barn behind the Bonaparte House. She made an attempt to escape and was shot dead in the garden area of the grounds. Residents of the apartments and the neighborhood have seen Chloris' ghostly apparition in the garden. There are also accounts of disembodied sobbing and moaning.

THE INN PHILADELPHIA

251–53 Camac Street

This business is no longer open.

The Inn was built in the heart of what was once Philadelphia's Red Light District. There are tunnels under the building, which are now believed to be the first part of the Underground Railroad. Two converted row houses now make up the structure of the restaurant.

Among the unexplained phenomena that occurs here are chandeliers swinging in a circular motion without a breeze or human interference, doors mysteriously opening, and a ghostly figure appearing on the second floor landing.

Very heavy, disembodied footsteps with a prominent limp have been heard. These are believed to be the owner's late father. He took an active role in the rebuilding process, wore very heavy work boots, and walked with a limp.

In the basement is a passageway believed to be a major stop on the Underground Railroad, on which slaves were brought from the south to Canada. Disembodied voices, noises and footsteps are often heard here, too.

PHILADELPHIA'S CITY HALL

BROAD AND MARKET STREETS

City Hall was built on William Penn's original Centre Square. It is the nation's largest and more than likely most ornate city hall. The tower contains four clocks and a 37-foot tall statue of William Penn, designed by Alexander Milne Calder, at the top. Mr. Penn, depending on the time of the year (and success of our sports teams) is sometimes "decked out" in a team jersey. I seriously doubt Mr. Calder had that in mind when he was designing and casting William Penn's statue. The Courtyard of City Hall has a very ornate tile pattern on the ground. It is also haunted…

Part of a chain gang killed an innocent local woman in her garden in front of her home near Centre Square. The "five wheelbarrow men," so called by Mr. Watson in *Annals of Philadelphia*, were executed. They were hanged on a common gallows where City Hall now stands.

There have been sightings of a dark Shadow Man swaying back and forth in the Courtyard. A Native American man, Joseph Hightower, was accused, found guilty, and convicted of murdering a Quaker family named Samuelson. He was also executed on the gallows. He proclaimed his innocence until his last breath. Right before dying, he swore he would avenge himself of this miscarriage of justice. Soon after his execution, James Mann, his arresting officer, drowned, and Robert Tanner, the prosecuting attorney, was run over by a carriage. The identity of the dark shadowy swaying figure still remains a mystery. Perhaps it is Joseph Hightower, or perhaps one of the wheelbarrow men or some other unfortunate soul hanged on the gallows at Centre Square.

SUPERNATURAL DATA: the gallows

In England, gallows were constructed at crossroads. This was done in the hope of confusing ghosts of the hanged people, just in case they decided to return to revisit those who took their lives.

Is it possible that our forefathers may have trapped the spirits of those executed on the gallows at Centre Square? It is where four roads (two more than a crossroads) meet and cease within the confines of the square. It seems as if there is one way in and no way out!

THE ACADEMY OF MUSIC

BROAD AND LOCUST STREETS

It was completed in 1857 and is often called the "Grande Old Lady of Locust Street." The building truly is a beautiful structure, ornate and attention paid to every detail. It has an enormous crystal chandelier and gas lamps, which were later wired for electricity. I have many wonderful memories of the Pennsylvania Ballet's *The Nutcracker* and many other shows here.

A mysterious specter, a man in black, is rumored to haunt the last row of seats in the upper balconies. He disappears when the light for intermission is shone. The majority of those who witnessed him found his presence "creepy." Some have called him scary. Unaccompanied female theater guests with empty seats next to them are often joined by an invisible escort for the duration of the performance. The seat seems to depress as if it is being occupied by an unseen patron. Some of the women have even been pinched by their invisible companion! If you are enjoying a performance at the Academy of Music, alone, and are a woman, you may want to drape your coat over the empty seat next to you. (Unless, of course, you want to be accompanied by an invisible escort in that empty chair next to you for the length of the show—but beware, your companion may get a little overzealous and pinch you!)

I hope you enjoyed your walking tour.

Part III

Unhaunted Sites... Or Are They?

Here is a small list of sites that are not haunted. Take photographs of these sites anyway, however. You never know—you may be the one to discover paranormal activity in one of these places. If you are a first time visitor to the City of Brotherly Love, you may want to check these sites out, too. Some of the sites have admission fees, while others are free.

THE LIBERTY BELL

LIBERTY BELL PLAZA IS AT 6TH AND MARKET STREETS, ACROSS FROM THE VISITOR'S CENTER.
THE LIBERTY BELL IS BETWEEN MARKET AND CHESTNUT STREETS.

THE NATIONAL CONSTITUTION CENTER

525 ARCH STREET, INDEPENDENCE MALL NORTH

This is an amazing, interactive place for adults and children alike. The exhibits here are astounding and interesting.

FRANKLIN SQUARE

6TH AND RACE STREETS

This is one of the coolest mini golf courses!

PHILADELPHIA HISTORY MUSEUM

7TH STREET, BELOW MARKET STREET
TUESDAY – SATURDAY, 10:30 – 4:30
FAMILY DISCOUNTS AVAILABLE; MILITARY PERSONNEL MAY ENTER FREE OF CHARGE

See more at www.philadelphiahistory.org

The entire museum is dedicated to the history of the city of Philadelphia!

SOUTH STREET

Between Lombard and Bainbridge Streets: start where Front Street meets South Street, walk, and enjoy. The shops and culture are for everyone, and the food is absolutely yummy, too.

HEAD HOUSE SQUARE

Between Spruce and Pine Streets, between 2nd and 3rd Streets. There is always some type of street fair or festival happening here. It will surely please everyone.

FRANKLIN INSTITUTE SCIENCE MUSEUM

22ND STREET AND BEN FRANKLIN PARKWAY

What can I say about this place except that it is a one-of-a-kind institution, like Mr. Franklin himself.

THE PHILADELPHIA ZOO

GIRARD AVENUE AND 34TH STREET, WEST FAIRMOUNT

No trip to the City of Brotherly love is complete without a visit to the Philadelphia Zoo. If you have not been here in a while, now is certainly the time to revisit this city treasure. It is also a national treasure, as it is the country's first zoo!

THE READING TERMINAL

12TH AND FILBERT STREET

This is one of my favorite places in Philadelphia. It has everything you could ever want, and a few things you would just love to try. This would probably be William Penn's favorite place, too. His dreams were of a city where different peoples lived in harmony and in religious freedom. Well, that harmony exists inside the Reading Terminal, in terms of food from everywhere, and it is just waiting to be eaten!

CHAPTER II

THE MUSEUM DISTRICT

THE SWANN FOUNTAIN

Logan Square

The Swann Fountain sits inside Logan Square, one of the four original squares designed by William Penn to frame Centre Square, City Hall. It was named after Mr. Penn's secretary, James Logan (more about Mr. Logan in Chapter Five) in 1825. The fountain was designed by Alexander Stirling Calder. His father, Alexander Milne Calder, designed the statue of William Penn atop City Hall.

The fountain represents the three waterways that frame the city: the Delaware River, Wissahickon Creek, and the Schuykill River. The Swann Fountain itself may be the stuff postcards are made of, but the grounds here have a very ominous history: it was once the site of a gallows and burial ground.

On February 7, 1803, convicted killer William Gross was executed here. His was the last execution to take place on these grounds. In addition, Logan Square was once a Potter's Field. Souls buried here range from American and British Revolutionary War Soldiers to criminals to those killed by the Yellow

Fever Epidemic, Native Americans, and, of course, the poor whose families were unable to provide proper burials.

Details of sightings here are sketchy at best: shadow figures, a strange mist, etc. I have to say, the energy on the grounds here is very strange. It is an excellent photo op location. On any given day (rain or shine) tourists and locals are snapping pictures here. In the summer months, this fountain is one of the most popular places in the city. Both adults and children gather around the fountain to cool off and enjoy a beautiful summer day, Philly style. Their energy is light, carefree and mostly pleasant.

However, there is a deeper current of energy, a kind of threatening dark energy below the surface. I have to confess, I scurry as quickly as possible whenever I pass through the square on my way to the public library. One evening, in the winter, I brought my pendulum and sat alone on one of the benches. While nothing specific materialized, I can testify there is definitely a dark, negative presence on these grounds. It magnifies at night. When the fountain is dry, the energy is particularly hostile. I think it is because there is no flow of water to disguise it or act as a buffer. I had to burn a great deal of sage and do many grounding exercises, along with an extra long meditation session just to remove the energy and return to my state of normal.

THE FREE LIBRARY
OF PHILADELPHIA

19TH AND VINE STREETS
OPEN SEVEN DAYS A WEEK; HOURS VARY

Walking through Logan Square, passing the Swann Fountain, following 19th Street, you will see the Free Library across Vine Street. It is a most impressive, classic-style building. Founded in 1891, this Central Branch of the Free Library of Philadelphia has more than one million volumes. The Rare Book room is the home of Ancient Sumerian clay tablets, first edition Dickens novels, and a variety of manuscripts, which include *The Raven* and *Murders in the Rue Morgue*.

There is also a volume of Pliny's Natural History, translated into Italian in 1476, from the first century A.D. It was Pliny the Younger, who reported one of the earliest ghost sightings in his letters. This occurred in the first century A.D.

One of the office staff told me the building was investigated by a local ghost hunter organization. While they did not witness anything specific in terms of ghosts or apparitions during their investigation, they did record

significant temperature changes and EMF (electro-magnetic field) activity in one of the boardrooms. A medium was also brought in on the investigation and reported sensing a few different, distinct energies throughout the building.

SUPERNATURAL DATA: cold spots

A cold spot is an indication that spirits are in close proximity. They absorb all the heat/energy out of the environment.

THE RODIN MUSEUM

23RD AND BENJAMIN FRANKLIN PARKWAY
OPEN TUESDAY – SUNDAY, 10 – 5   DONATION SUGGESTED

Traveling to the Rodin Museum requires negotiating circles and some creative motoring, if driving. Sound crazy? Then just walk up the Benjamin Franklin Parkway from 19th Street to 23rd Street toward the Philadelphia Museum of Art. Before you run up those steps, like Rocky, take a little detour.

The Rodin Museum houses the best collection of the works of Auguste Rodin outside of France. You will see his immortal classics such as *The Thinker* and *The Kiss*, and you will also pass through *The Gates of Hell.* The gardens are most beautiful in spring when everything is in full bloom.

The Rodin Museum was a gift to the City of Philadelphia from Jules Mastbaum. Mr. Mastbaum was a movie mogul and native Philadelphian. This was his own collection of the works of August Rodin. He commissioned French-American architect Paul Philippe Cret and French landscape architect Jacques Greber to design a Beaux Arts building and formal garden to display it, all for the "enjoyment of my fellow citizens."

Then there is the ghost story—a story of star-crossed lovers, Philadelphia style. The gardens of the museum are believed to be haunted. The following account of events may be the reason why:

Her name was Rachel, and she was from a very well-to-do, upper-class family in Rittenhouse. Her father was a distinguished physician. Her boyfriend's name was Hank, and he was from the working class neighborhood of Brewerytown, in the city—the wrong side of the tracks, so to speak.

None of this mattered to Rachel and Hank. They did have two things in common: they both shared a love of the works of art in the museum and gardens, and they loved each other. Rachel's father was less than enthusiastic about the situation. Upon discovering her secret love, he sent her away to boarding school in upstate New York. He believed Hank was beneath them and hoped the separation would be the end of the relationship.

Two years of school passed, and summers in Europe kept her far away from Philadelphia. Rachel served out her time in boarding school like a prison sentence. As soon as she was able to return to Philadelphia, she began searching for Hank. She began her search at the Rodin Museum and then went to his home in Brewerytown, only to find it boarded up. A neighbor told her Hank had been sent to Vietnam, where he was killed in action. His mother passed away soon after. Rachel returned to the Rodin Museum. Overwhelmed with depression, despair and sadness, she ran into the path of oncoming traffic. She was struck and killed immediately in front of the museum's gardens.

There have been sightings reported from both locals and tourists. They see a ghostly couple in the gardens, very much in love, in death as in life. They are seen cuddling on one of the benches and suddenly vanish into thin air. These sightings have been consistent and are recent as well.

THE JOAN of ARC STATUE

Joan of Arc sits on her horse, prepared for battle, on the Benjamin Franklin Parkway. She is forever young, courageous, and beautiful. It is difficult to miss this huge gold statue. Plus, there is a frightfully eerie story behind the creation of it.

On January 6, 1412, Joan of Arc was born in the village of Domremy la Pucelle. She defeated the British (and their monarch), drove them from France, and established the Dauphin to the throne of France. She accomplished this all before the ripe old age of seventeen. On May 30, 1431, she was burned at the stake, convicted of being a heretic and blasphemer.

In 1898, Emanuel Fremets sculpted the statue of Joan of Arc. His model was a girl named Valerie Laneau. She was fifteen years old, and from the same village, Domrémy-la-Pucelle, as Joan. Coincidentally, she and Joan shared the same birthday, January 6th. Here's the really eerie part: Valerie, like Joan, died as the result of being engulfed, or consumed, by fire. Joan was burned at the stake, and her death was an intentional execution. Valerie was engulfed by flames in a mishap with an oil lamp and burned to death as a result of the accident. Valerie's unfortunate death occurred on May 30th, the same day Joan of Arc was executed.

THE PHILADELPHIA
MUSEUM of ART

Cross the Benjamin Franklin Parkway and you will be on the side of the Philadelphia Museum of Art, which houses over 2000 years of human creativity. All periods and styles are represented, and their visiting exhibits are nothing less than amazing.

If you bear left, you can move to the front of the building, where you will see the imposing Art Museum steps, which are almost as famous as the building itself. They were immortalized in the film *Rocky* in the 1970s. Every Mother's Day, breast cancer survivors promenade down them in a victory walk/strut. It is truly an awe inspiring sight, one that will evoke twice as many goose pimples as any ghost sighting!

There is also a camera shy entity in the Elizabethan Room. In December of 1997, a woman, a tourist from Germany, was in the Elizabethan Room admiring the works of art on display. Then, she was suddenly slapped in the face. However, no one was close to the woman. Here's where it gets really interesting: upon viewing the film footage from the security cameras, only the woman is on film. No living beings, human or otherwise, were in the vicinity of the tourist. Her face visibly contorts and her neck snaps back, as if she is being struck by some invisible force.

Historical Data:
The Benjamin Franklin Parkway

The Benjamin Franklin Parkway is often called the Champs-Élysées of Philadelphia. It was fashioned after the famous Boulevard in Paris, and contains fountains, museums, and statues, including Joan of Arc—only it's Philadelphia, not Paris. Plus, the Benjamin Franklin Parkway was named after the city's most famous citizen, who also happened to be an ambassador to France.

FAIRMOUNT WATER WORKS

OFF THE BENJAMIN FRANKLIN PARKWAY,
BEHIND THE PHILADELPHIA MUSEUM OF ART

Walking around to the back of the Art Museum will lead you to a path and an open air black iron observatory. There, you will have an amazing view of the Waterworks, Boat House Row, and the Schuykill River. Following the very steep path (not recommended for high heels, but runners love it) will lead you directly to the Fairmount Water Works.

It is a national, historic, and civil landmark, all rolled up into one impressive package. It is also on the National Register of Historic Places. Frederick Graff, expert on hydraulic engineering, created a new system of the delivery and management of water. Completed in 1822, the building included a mill, a pump house and reservoir, a superintendent's house, pavilions, and balustrades along the river. An interesting fact, the Water Works Museum is below ground.

The ghost of Edgar Allan Poe visits this site. Like Benjamin Franklin, Mr. Poe seems to have a very active afterlife. Sightings of Edgar Allan Poe place him on the walkway surrounding the Water Works. His spirit is visibly restless, troubled, upset, and sometimes seems confused. He moves in an erratic pattern, much like the walks he took in the same area, close to the end of his life. The ghost of Benjamin Franklin has also been reported strolling around the grounds and enjoying the view of the Water Works.

The day I visited this site was a strange day. The weather was unsettled at best. It was spring, but the day itself was grey, dismal and very chilly for the season. I kept looking to the sky, waiting for it to open and pour rain on me while I photographed the area. The energy of the area was just as unsettled. I would not have been surprised to see Edgar Allan Poe's ghost at any given moment. The dark, damp day would have provided the perfect setting and conditions to see Edgar in his troubled, confused, and agitated state. I could not get any kind of a reading from my pendulum: not accurate nor even transitional. It was highly influenced by the confusion in the air. My pendulum was answering questions—just not the ones I was asking it at that particular time. All in all, it was a very peculiar day and a learning experience.

Across the Schuylkill River from the Fairmount Water Works is Philadelphia's famous Boat House Row. It is definitely an excellent photo opportunity, day or night, but it is most impressive in the evening when the houses are lit up.

Before the famous Boat Houses, the Fairmount Water Works, and the picturesque Art Museum were created, giving the city its unforgettable view of the Schuykill, there were pirates! It is rumored that there is pirate treasure buried along the banks of the Schuykill River. I believe anything is possible, but I just have one very important question. Where should I start digging?

The Lenape/Lenapi Indians also have stories of supernatural beings and phantom lights along the Schuykill River. Stories of ghost lights along the Schuykill River date back to the Colonial Era. Sightings of these Phantom lights dancing across the river have been consistent from Colonial days to the present.

SUPERNATURAL DATA: phantom lights

Phantom lights or ghost lights are considered to be a paranormal phenomenon when lights cannot be explained by ordinary means. The lights are often called St. Elmo's Fire (no relation to the movie whatsoever).

The Lantern Men were believed to be shadow spirits who used their light(s) to lure travelers from the pathways into the marshes to drown them.

THE MUTTER MUSEUM

THE COLLEGE OF PHYSICIANS OF PHILADELPHIA
19 SOUTH 22ND STREET
OPEN DAILY, 10 – 5   THERE IS AN ADMISSION FEE FOR THIS SITE

The Mutter Museum was founded in 1849 at the suggestion of Dr. Isaac Parrish of the College of Physicians of Philadelphia. It was named after Dr. Thomas Dent Mutter, the museum's first benefactor. He donated cash endowments as well as his own personal collection of instructive anatomical and pathological specimens. The collection continues to grow. It houses "normal items," but it is known for its collection of medical oddities. These oddities include Anatomist Joseph Hyrtl's collection of skulls, President Grover Cleveland's facial tumor, and a piece of the thorax of President Lincoln's assassin, John Wilkes Booth. It is also the home of the mysterious "Soap Woman," who died sometime during the 1800s. She was buried in the vicinity of 4th and Race Streets, and her body literally turned to soap. Her identity and cause of death still remain a mystery.

THE ROSENBACH MUSEUM AND LIBRARY

2010 DELANCEY PLACE   THERE IS AN ADMISSION FEE FOR THIS SITE

There is a collection of stationery here from the Bellevue Stratford Hotel, handwritten by Bram Stoker. The subject of these pages is not surprising: vampires and werewolves.

While neither the Mutter Museum nor the Rosenbach Museum and Library are haunted, they are extremely cool places and well worth a visit.

CHAPTER III

SUPERNATURAL LEGENDS AND HISTORIC GHOSTS

THE CAVE OF KELPIUS

This is one of my favorite Philadelphia legends. It has everything that makes a legend exciting and supernatural: a little likeness to the tale of King Arthur, a little Harry Potter, and even the end of the world!

The Cave of Kelpius is located on Forbidden Drive. There is a pedestrian walk beside the Wissahickon Creek, and if you walk through the woods near Hermit Lane (not Hermit Street or Hermit Terrace), the cave is not far from the creek. In 1961, the Rosicrucian Society erected a monument beside the stone hut/cave. Today, there is a Pennsylvania Historical Marker that commemorates the Brotherhood of Kelpius.

Friar Johannes Kelpius is believed to have meditated in solitude, away from the other monks. The twenty-one-year-old Kelpius, a priest/monk, member of the brotherhood of German Mystics, who practiced medicine, magic, and alchemy in the Wissahickon Woods in the Fairmount Park section of the city near Wissahickon Creek, lived in a cave, in seclusion.

This brotherhood tended to the sick and helped all people regardless of their religious persuasion in Philadelphia and Germantown. They had many names, which included the Rosicrucian Society and the Women of the Wilderness (from the Book of Revelation in the Holy Bible). The brotherhood stayed in their cave, waiting for the end of the world, a.k.a. the Rapture. They used telescopes and astro-blades to chart and look for signs. They also practiced Astrology and Numerology.

On June 23rd, the eve of St. John the Baptist Day, around the summer solstice, they celebrated with a festival and made use of a tabernacle with a cross within a heart—a Rosicrucian symbol. It was believed they had visions of angels during this festival.

Kelpius developed pneumonia, undoubtedly the result of wintering in a cave in Pennsylvania. In 1708, the virus became terminal. As the legend states, on his deathbed, Johannes Kelpius presented his assistant Daniel Gessler with a locked box filled with magical artifacts. There was a note with instructions to throw the box into the Schuykill River immediately—just like King Arthur demanding Excalibur return to the Lady of the Lake.

So, Arthur entrusted Sir Bedivere with the task. He had been Arthur's loyal servant since Arthur removed Excalibur from the infamous stone. Sir Bedivere hid Excalibur on the shores of the lake. Daniel Gessler, like Sir Bedivere, did not follow the instructions. He believed the contents of the box would be too valuable for future generations. Instead, he hid the box on the banks of the Schuykill and returned to Kelpius.

Like King Arthur, Kelpius knew his request had been disobeyed. He then sternly ordered Gessler to throw the box into the Schuykill. Gessler returned to the banks of the Schuykill and did as he was told. As the box hit the water, explosions of lightning and thunder occurred. Many believe this box contained the famous Philosopher's Stone (made renown by the first *Harry Potter* movie).

If the Philosopher's Stone does in fact exist, one possibility is that it lies at the bottom of the Schuykill River. I must admit, I cannot imagine putting on the scuba gear and diving for it. After Kelpius's death, the brotherhood's numbers diminished, but the remaining monks still provided services to the community. It was claimed that one of the monks, Conrad Matthai, could cast out demons and travel outside his body (a.k.a. astral projection), along with his regular duties as a monk.

After dark, especially late at night, while walking the trails next to the Wissahickon Creek, you may encounter six ghostly hiking partners. They wear brown hooded robes, like Kelpius, and are as faithful in death as in life to him.

Just for the record, (contrary to the Harry Potter *movies) Nicolas Flamel most likely did not give the Philosopher's Stone to Johannes Kelpius. The French alchemist died in 1418. He still remains somewhat of a mythic figure, even though he is an actual historical person, too.*

Historical Data:
Ancient Philadelphia

Philadelphia not only means the City of Brotherly Love—it also comes from William Penn's reading of the Book of Revelation (in the Holy Bible). It speaks of a faithful church in the ancient, Middle Eastern city of Philadelphia.

"We are waiting for the end of the world...dear Lord, I sincerely hope you're coming because you really started something." – Elvis Costello

BENJAMIN FRANKLIN

Mr. Benjamin Franklin is probably the most beloved and colorful of all the Founding Fathers. Born on January 17, 1706, in Boston, Massachusetts, he had no formal education beyond the age of 10—he was completely self taught. At the age of 16, he arrived in Philadelphia, alone, to fulfill his destiny.

His accomplishments were numerous: clerk of the Pennsylvania Assembly, Post Master of Philadelphia, then of all the colonies, member to both First and Second Continental Congresses, and Ambassador to the French Court. Incidentally, he was loved as much in France as here in Philadelphia. It was most likely because of his charm and the fact that he made himself accessible to the French people.

He was a writer, publisher, diplomat, scientist, legislator, and social activist. He also founded the Academy of Natural Sciences and the Library Company of Philadelphia, and published Poor Richard's Almanac. A little known fact is that he introduced tofu to the colonies. He sent soybeans with instructions to John Bartram, who planted them in his garden in Germantown.

Mr. Franklin also loved female companionship. It is believed he fathered 68 children before his death on April 17, 1790. During his lifetime, Mr. Franklin was the rock star of Philadelphia and considered one of its most famous residents.

Mr. Franklin is most likely our most famous ghost, too! These days, he is just as much the Renaissance man, albeit it a supernatural Renaissance man, as in the early days of our country. Every Easter Sunday, in the early hours of the morning, the bronze statue of Mr. Franklin detaches itself from Library Hall. Located across 5th Street from the American Philosophical Society, his ghostly statue dances across the sidewalk. His ghost has also been sighted in the same vicinity, walking swiftly and carrying an armful of books.

In 1881, a Philadelphia newspaper article reported Benjamin Franklin's ghost had pinched the backside of a cleaning woman in Library Hall. She fell in terror upon seeing his ghost. Perhaps she should have lectured Mr. Franklin on his poor manners like the other cleaning woman in Library Hall. His ghost seems to avoid confrontation of any type, especially negative, with women. To date, attractive women in Library Hall are often mysteriously fondled and grasped. Apparently, Mr. Franklin's fondness of female companionship continues into his afterlife!

His ghost also strolls through Franklin Court, through the skeleton frame of what was once his home. Finally, Benjamin Franklin's ghostly apparition is also fond of strolling around the Fairmount Water Works. His ghost has been sighted taking a casual walk in the area, just as he did in life.

Historical Data:
Hessian Mercenaries

The British Crown, King George III, paid Germanic princes seven English pounds for each mercenary Hessian soldier they offered to fight in the Revolutionary War against the Colonies. Seven pounds per head was the popular reference of the day. This may be the reason why so many Hessian soldiers were decapitated by the Patriots (mentioned later in Allens Lane, the General Wayne Inn, and the Headless Horseman Legend).

Also, Benjamin Franklin wrote a satirical essay in which he tried to sell back the remaining Hessians who were hiding in the Colonies after the Revolutionary War. In his essay, "The Sale of the Hessians," Mr. Franklin demands 483,450 florins for the soldiers. He also wished to make a profit on them. Somehow, only Mr. Franklin could get away with something so incredibly gutsy. The following quote from the essay says it all:

"The Court of London objects that there were a hundred wounded who ought not to be included in the list, nor paid for as dead...and that you will not have tried by human succor to recall the life of the unfortunates whose days could not be lengthened but by the loss of a leg or an arm...I do not mean you should assassinate them; we should be humane, but you may insinuate to the surgeons with entire propriety that a crippled man is a reproach to their profession, and that there is no wiser course than to let every one of them die when he ceases to be fit to fight."

EDGAR ALLAN POE

Edgar Allan Poe wrestled with complex psychological issues and demons his entire life. The recurring instances of separation and desertion, sorrow, and desperation, coupled with mistreatment from his adopted father, plagued him from early childhood to his untimely death. They shaped his character, darkened his moods, at times clouded his judgment, and undoubtedly influenced his writing style.

He was born on January 19, 1809, in Boston, Massachusetts. When his parents separated, he was adopted by the wealthy Mr. and Mrs. John Allan. As a child, he was schooled in London, returned to America, and began studies at the University of Virginia in 1826. He had to leave school after a year because of mounting debts, and John Allan refused to help him financially. This made it impossible for Edgar to attend the university; he could not concentrate on his studies and financially support himself. (No student, at this time, could do both.)

In 1827, he went to Boston and joined the army. Surprisingly, Edgar did well as a soldier. He was accepted into West Point but had to leave after a year. Again, he had mounting debts, and again John Allan refused to help him. In 1831, he moved on to New York City, where he married this 13-year-old cousin, Virginia Clemm.

Some of his poetry was published at this time, but his short stories were rejected. He began a career as an editor. In 1828, he came to Philadelphia, and wrote *Ligeia* and *The Haunted Palace* and his first volume of short stories, entitled *Tales of the Grotesque and Arabesque*. He was quite successful as an editor, and started his own magazine, *The Stylus*, which failed. He also published *The Murders in the Rue Morgue* and *The Gold Bug*.

In 1847, Virginia Clemm died and Edgar collapsed from stress and recovered. He returned to Philadelphia in June 1849 to visit a friend, John Sartain. Sartain documented the event because of Edgar's erratic behavior. This is where it gets a little strange. It is almost as if the Greek god of Tragedy was controlling Edgar's destiny. He left Philadelphia, intending to travel to Richmond, Virginia. He then returned to Philadelphia with the intent of traveling to New York City. However, he boarded the wrong train and ended up in Baltimore, Maryland.

On October 31, 1849, Edgar Allan Poe was found lying in a gutter, wearing someone else's clothes. He was taken to a hospital, where he drifted in and out of consciousness, never being able to tell what had happened to him. Edgar's death has been blamed on a variety of things which include alcoholism and drug use, rabies, a seizure, and even murder.

After a recent visit to the Edgar Allan Poe National Historic Site, I've learned that new light has been shed on Edgar's untimely death. The park ranger informed us of new information that was "unearthed," so to speak: Edgar's body had been exhumed recently, and something was "rattling around" in his skull. Since the brain eventually evaporates, it is believed the thing that rattled inside Edgar's skull was a calcified cancerous brain tumor. Brain cancer would definitely explain his erratic behavior.

In addition to the new medical evidence, some environmental information has surfaced as well, which might shed new light on his death. Edgar was staying at Gunnar's Hall (a notoriously deviant polling place) on Election Day, and is believed to have been a victim of "cooping" (a derivative of the phrase, "being cooped up"), which explains why he was not wearing his own clothes. Cooping was practiced by corrupt people/politicians. Unsuspecting men were kidnapped, forced into a room above the polling place and made to vote, then probably beaten and given a lot of liquor. They switched clothes, voted again, and were either beaten again or given more liquor. This vicious cycle was repeated, and the men were held until the following morning. Edgar was already in a fragile state, both mentally and physically, and his body could not tolerate the trauma inflicted by the corrupt, evil men. He most likely passed on as a direct result of those actions. I can only hope and believe that, in death, he has finally found the peace he deserves.

Like the ghosts of General Anthony Wayne and George Washington, Edgar Allan Poe's ghost crosses state lines. He haunts locations in Pennsylvania, Maryland, and Virginia. Perhaps most notoriously, Mr. Poe haunts the infamous General Wayne Inn. (The Inn's supernatural history and bloody past will be discussed later.) He dined and wrote there in 1839, preferred the same room in which Benjamin Franklin delivered the mail, and always sat at the same table near the window. It was believed he edited or wrote part of *The Raven* at that very table. He carved his initials, "EAP," in the window glass using a diamond ring he borrowed from his friend, Henry Beck Hirst. The window remained unharmed until the 1970s.

Edgar's ghost takes on two appearances. He is dressed in his usual black suit, like in his portrait, and he is also seen in his cadet uniform. In either wardrobe, he appears very tired and spent. There are a couple of sightings of Edgar standing close to his portrait, pointing at it and laughing.

Edgar also haunts his residence on Amity Street in Baltimore, Maryland. Paranormal activity dates back to the 1960s, with disembodied hushed voices, windows and doors opening by themselves, and phantom hands touching visitors' shoulders. The majority of the activity comes from Edgar's attic room. The rumors have circulated that the house is protected from the local street gangs by Edgar's ghost—they call him "Mr. Eddie."

Westminster Churchyard is located a few blocks from the house on Amity Street. Edgar Allan Poe is buried here, and his grave is the site of an unusual occurrence. It began in 1944: a mysterious, dark figure swoops down on Edgar's grave, leaving three red roses and a bottle of cognac. The man/figure wears a black, cape, or cloak, and fedora. His scarf hides his face. People wait to see him, and he eludes them all the time.

In 1990, *LIFE* magazine sent a photographer with night vision equipment. The results were as follows: a man was captured on film, kneeling at Edgar Allan Poe's grave, but no identifiable facial features were visible. No one seems to know if this is actually Edgar's ghost or simply an admirer.

In Fort Monroe, Virginia, Edgar haunts the Old Fort Monroe and Case Mate Museum, specifically Building No. 5. Edgar wanders through the area of his old barracks. Interestingly, he gave a poetry reading here one month before he died.

Finally, the Talavera House in Richmond, Virginia seems to be haunted by Edgar Allan Poe's ghost. Thomas Talley built the house in 1838, and Edgar visited his daughter, Susan, there on several occasions. One evening, Susan gave an absolutely horrifying reading of *The Raven*, and all the servants ran out of the house. Edgar died two weeks after that reading. It has only been rumored that Talavera is haunted by Edgar's ghost: the proof has not yet been substantiated.

GENERAL ANTHONY WAYNE

Although there are no official or unofficial recorded sightings of General Wayne in the city of Philadelphia, his story and legend was just too cool to omit.

Anthony Wayne was a general in the Revolutionary War and was awarded the title "Mad Anthony" from the men he commanded. His fiery temper and fearless activity on the battlefield were undoubtedly the reasons. He survived the Revolutionary War and went on to fight the Indians in Michigan. He died in 1796, in Erie, Pennsylvania, while returning home. Thirteen years later, Gen. Wayne's son, Isaac decided to return his father's body to the family plot in Chester County, Pennsylvania. However, the citizens of Erie wanted the General to remain there.

A very strange compromise then occurred. Dr. James Wallace boiled Gen. Wayne's body, removing all of the flesh from his bones. His flesh and clothing were then re-buried in Erie. Isaac was given his father's bones to return home to bury in the family plot in Chester County. The chest containing the General's bones was not properly locked and some fell off the back of the wagon as it traveled. Isaac buried the remaining bones in St. David's Cemetery.

The legend/story goes, every New Year's Day, in the early morning hours, the ghost of General Mad Anthony Wayne rides the road between Erie and Chester County Pennsylvania in search of his missing bones. The road is now US 322.

Mad Anthony is a traveling spirit. His ghost has been seen in various locations in the colonies. Other reported Pennsylvania sightings include seeing the Phantom General on his horse riding through the battlefield at Valley Forge National Military Park, and sighting his ghost near his memorial statue at Brandywine Battlefield.

In New York, his apparition is reported in Stony Point and at Fort Ticonderoga. In Stony Point, the General's ghost rides through the tunnels and woods on his horse. Blue and orange sparks fly from the horse's hooves when they hit the pavement. This particular apparition of the General is only seen on dark and stormy nights. At Fort Ticonderoga, the General is seen in the Commandant's dining room, seated in a chair near the fire place.

In the "spirit" of colonial ghostly gossip, the ghost of Anthony Wayne's lover, Nancy Coates has been reported here, too. Her apparition roams the grounds of Fort Ticonderoga at night. Nancy committed suicide by drowning herself in the lake at the Fort. She did this after General Wayne ceased his relationship with her and began pursuing a British girl. His ghost is also seen at Lake Memphremagog, Vermont. This sighting is unusual because his apparition is dressed as an Indian scout gliding across the lake with his arms extended at his sides and an eagle perched on each hand.

BENEDICT ARNOLD

Benedict Arnold is most famous for being an infamous traitor to his country; he is quite different from the patriots and Founding Fathers. Amidst his military service and personal health sacrifices (a horrible leg injury), his loyalties remained only to himself.

Born in 1741 in Norwich, Connecticut, to a wealthy family, their financial circumstances changed greatly due to poor business ventures. Young Arnold was often in trouble because he did not go to school, and his mother and father were not the hands-on parenting type. His cousins took him on as an apprentice in their apothecary business. He fought in the French and Indian War and retired to New Haven, Connecticut, when the war was over. Retirement consisted of shady business dealings, like smuggling.

In 1767, he married Margaret Mansfield and had three sons. His military service took him to Canada. He attempted to take Quebec, but was outnumbered, the weather was brutally against him, and most of his men contracted smallpox. Arnold himself was injured and on his sickbed. General George Washington admired his tenacity and made him a Brigadier General. He was sent to Montreal, where he plundered and was almost court-martialed. His rank was taken from him, which left him enraged and embittered.

He spent the infamous winter of 1777-1778 with General Washington in Valley Forge, where he signed an oath of allegiance. His bitterness and resentment was increasing because his seniority was not restored.

Arnold arrived in the city of Philadelphia during the British occupation. He was a widower then, and married the very young and pretty Peggy Shippen. She came from a family of rich British loyalists. The couple lived well beyond their means, and Arnold began his shady business dealings again. This time he was court martialed for his actions.

It was at this time Arnold decided to strike a deal with the British Army. He would assist them in taking West Point Military Academy. Why would a man who was so tenacious in fighting the British turn around and betray his country to them? Maybe Arnold only cared for his own glory, vanity, liberty, and freedom. His priorities, unlike his contemporaries, revolved around his ego and anything benefiting him. He would most likely be called a sociopath today.

Benedict Arnold lived out his final days in London, where he was received with apathy instead of glory. He died a bitter, resentful man, much the way he lived.

One question comes to mind: why does Benedict Arnold's ghost haunt sites in the city of Philadelphia? Only Benedict Arnold knows for sure. We can only speculate. One theory is that he is so full of bitterness and negativity, he is (karmically) forced to relive his seedy, traitorous days.

Another theory states he returns to this city to make right what he made wrong. Yet another theory is that he was happy and very much in love with his pretty young wife and returns to happier days as a ghost. Only Benedict Arnold knows for sure. The fact that Arnold haunts Independence Hall can be the result of his spirit having unfinished business in the "Cradle of Liberty." However, both Arnold's apparition and that of his wife, Peggy Shippen, have been reported at the Powel House, where they attended parties. This suggests he wishes to seek happier days. Like I said before, only Benedict Arnold knows for sure.

THOMAS JEFFERSON

Born on April 13, 1743, Thomas Jefferson, like his contemporary Benjamin Franklin, was a true Renaissance man, but also modest, shy, and unpretentious. Mr. Jefferson was educated at the College of William and Mary, where he studied law. He was fluent in five languages and could read and write in two additional ones.

Thomas Jefferson represented the state of Virginia at the Continental Congress. His theories regarding self-government were published in the article, "A Summary View of the Rights of British America." In 1776, he was chosen by the committee to write a draft of the Declaration of Independence. It was adopted, of course, on July 4, 1776.

In 1781, he retired to Monticello to write and work on improved agriculture. He accompanied Mr. Franklin to France as American Diplomats in 1784. In 1796, he ran for president against John Adams, but lost. So, he became Vice President. This was extremely difficult for Mr. Jefferson because they constantly disagreed on governing. He also found Mr. Adams's personality very harsh and judgmental. Also, he believed Mr. Adams's political views on governing were directly opposite his.

His experiences as Vice President directly influenced him to create the 12th Amendment, the manner in which a Vice President is selected. He also wrote an article that established the standard of weights and measures in America.

As the third President of the United States, he was responsible for the Louisiana Purchase. In 1800, he established the Library of Congress by selling his own personal book collection to Congress. Mr. Jefferson was an agronomist, musician, author, scientist, inventor, philosopher and statesman. He and close friend James Madison (4th President and Dolley's husband) established the University of Virginia.

Mr. Jefferson died on July 4, 1826. Coincidentally, John Adams died the same day. He said he only wanted to be remembered for two things: the Declaration of Independence and establishing the University of Virginia.

Mr. Jefferson's ghost has been seen in the formal dining room in Baleroy Mansion in Chestnut Hill.

GEORGE WASHINGTON

George Washington was born in 1732 in Westmoreland County, Virginia. His father died when he was only three years old. So, his older brother, Laurence, became a major influence on his character, teaching him trigonometry, surveying, and ethics. Laurence also encouraged young George's love of reading novels, music, and the theater.

Another influence on young George was the wealthy Fairfax family, not to mention the crush he had on Sally Fairfax. Lord Fairfax sent him to survey the Shenandoah Valley for a month. He was then appointed surveyor of Culpeper City. Both Laurence and George contracted smallpox: Laurence died at Mt. Vernon, and George survived the disease, gaining immunity to it and inheriting Mt. Vernon. He eventually married Martha Custas, a wealthy widow with land and two children, after Sally Fairfax married another man.

In May of 1753, he got into skirmishes with the French along the Ohio River. During the French Indian War, George Washington was promoted to Colonel and given command over all Virginia forces. At this time, he began to harbor resentment toward the British.

In 1774, George Washington signed a resolve proposing a Continental Congress and the ban of imported British goods. He was sent to the First

Continental Congress and returned home to organize individual militia companies in northern Virginia. In 1775, he was sent to the Second Continental Congress, where he was given command over the American Forces. He took no pay for this commission. General Washington and the Continental Army suffered through an ungodly winter at Valley Forge in 1777-78. He crossed the Delaware River early Christmas morning to surprise the British troops in Trenton. Victories at Yorktown and New York followed.

He was unanimously elected the first President of the United States, taking his oath of office on April 30, 1789. On September 19, 1796, George Washington gave his farewell address as President of the United States, and in December 1799, after an evening ride around Mt. Vernon, George Washington died.

Our First President was visited by an angel. At least he perceived the visitation to have been from an angel or at the very least something divine. He was at the height of his despair (depression) during the wickedly bitter winter of 1777. He sank into despair over his military defeats coupled with the utter brutality of the winter. His men/soldiers were shoeless and hungry. It was in this hour an angel appeared to General Washington, giving him the message to continue to fight as a "Son of the Republic." Thank heavens (or the angel) he did as she said, and the rest is history. This incident has been recorded in letters from the president. The fact that he actually recorded the happening may prove Our First President was in his own special way a spiritualist.

In Washington, D.C., the ghosts of both George and Martha Washington have been sighted in the Pension Building in Judiciary Square. George Washington also haunts his home at Mt. Vernon. This is not surprising, because our first president loved his home and being a farmer there.

The following is another account of an appearance of General Washington's ghost. I can easily say this is not something anyone will forget. In July 1863, in Gettysburg, Pennsylvania, the ghost of General George Washington appeared to the Union Troops the night before the bloodiest battle of the Civil War.

He was on his horse wearing his tri-cornered hat and glowing. Hundreds of men witnessed this glowing apparition of General Washington. The Union Army even launched a formal investigation at the request of Edwin Stanton, the Secretary of War. General Oliver Hunt and many other Union officers swore that the apparition had the face of General George Washington. Colonel Joshua Chamberlain from Maine (a scholar and college professor, not a military or West Point man) was directly in charge of all the troops who witnessed General Washington's glowing ghost and had this to say:

> "We know not what mystic power may be possessed by those who are now bivouacking with the dead. I only know the effect, but I dare not explain or deny the cause. Who shall say that Washington was not among the number of those who aided the country that he founded?"

Memorials, flowers and other symbols of respect and admiration, to this day, are left in the exact spot where Colonel Chamberlain held the Union line and did not allow the Confederate soldiers to break it. I have visited Gettysburg several times over the years: I have to say, while the entire battlefield is hallowed ground, that specific place on the battlefield is awe inspiring.

General George Washington's crossing of the Delaware River is re-enacted every Christmas morning, around 6 a.m. It is done at Washington's Crossing National Park, and should be on every American's "bucket list" of things to witness. It really is a sight to be seen!

SUPERNATURAL DATA: unfinished business

According to Maureen Wood, in her book *A Ghost a Day*, there are four reasons a ghost stays on our earthly plane: (1) he or she is unaware of his/her death; (2) the individual has unfinished business with the living, perhaps a family member; (3) the individual has a strong desire to say goodbye to loved ones; and (4) the individual has an overwhelming desire to provide guidance to a living loved one.

Our Founding Fathers are still here in the City of Brotherly Love, which is strangely comforting. It is almost as if we have guardian angels of liberty and freedom watching over our historic sites and us. In places like Carpenter's Hall and Independence Hall, where disembodied ghostly voices of many men have been heard arguing, we are unsure as to exactly whom is speaking. Is it Benjamin Franklin or Thomas Jefferson or the very boisterous John Adams?

Who are the unknown apparitions and spirits at Independence Hall who only show up in photographs? Is it John Adams or George Washington or Benjamin "rock star" Franklin? These are things that are yet to be discovered. Perhaps one of us will have an answer to these questions. One thing I do know is that I look forward to the search for these answers, and I am very excited about the results of future visits and sessions.

CHAPTER IV

SUPERNATURAL AND GHOST STORIES FROM THE SURROUNDING AREA

THE MARTIN HOUSE

CAMDEN, NEW JERSEY

This tenement building has been torn down. It was located at 522 North 5th Avenue, in Camden, which is across the Delaware River from Philadelphia. This 60-year-old, three story tenement building was haunted by two ghosts for almost thirty years. The apparitions of a woman and her small son appeared to generations of the Martin family, who lived in this house for over three decades. Family members reported the ghost of the boy who played with the Martin children. On occasion, the ghostly little boy even climbed into bed with them at night.

Many paranormal experts believe that most children are susceptible or receptive to seeing spirits prior to the age of seven.

OLD LAWSON PLACE

VINCENTOWN, NEW JERSEY

The ruins of the granite/stone house can be found in the Locust Grove area outside Vincentown. Lawson Place was once the home of Alta Cossart Lawson. Alta's family settled there in the 1840s. The family was originally from Austria. She ran both of her husband's businesses: an iron foundry and shipyards.

She was unyielding and ruled with the proverbial iron fist. She was also what we would refer to as a compulsive spender: the businesses were lost and the family fell into poverty. The house fell into shambles, but Alta continued to live there after her husband died with her son, Lambert, and his wife.

One night in 1890, the nightmarish tension drove Lambert into a fit of rage. He attacked his wife with an ax. She tried to escape, but he decapitated her. Her skull rolled down the steps into the yard. Lambert was taken to an insane asylum. Alta died in severe poverty in the house a few years later. Her ghost is often seen in the ruins of the old house, taking an evening walk on the property. She is finely dressed in a purple silk gown with a bonnet full of ostrich feathers. No doubt she is reliving her wealthier, happier days. Lambert Lawson's enraged apparition is also seen on the grounds.

BURLINGTON COUNTY PRISON

HIGH STREET, BURLINGTON, NEW JERSEY

A cell on the third floor of the prison is haunted by the presence of an inmate named Joseph Clough. He was imprisoned there in the 1850s, convicted of murder—he beat his mistress to death with a table leg. Clough was chained to the floor of Cell Five for the duration of his stay, before he was put to death by hanging. Sounds are heard coming from Cell Five. The sounds of heavy chains moving and moaning are believed to be Clough. Sometimes inmates see cigarettes floating in mid air. Many guards have reported feeling a presence in the cell when no one is there.

SEVEN STARS TAVERN

Woodstown, Salem County, New Jersey

This is no longer a tavern. It is now a private residence on the corner of Kings Highway and Woodstown-Auburn Road. Please be respectful when photographing.

The Seven Stars Tavern was built in 1762 and was once referred to as the most haunted house in New Jersey. Noisy ghosts are heard climbing stairs. Some of the spirits sound as if they are arguing with each other. They even have physical (as physical as the dead can get) altercations, pushing and shoving each other.

In the 1930s, some of the farm workers witnessed an absolutely horrendous sight. The apparition of a man with a noose around his neck appeared to them one night. Ungodly sounds came from him and blood poured from his mouth. He gestured to the noose, obviously wanting someone to take it from his neck. The man was hanged from an attic beam. Popular belief was that he was a Tory spy and obviously punished for his loyalty to the British Crown.

THE DAVY ESTATE

The mansion is in horrible decay. It is located not far from Temple University, in an area that was originally part of Wright's Farm.

The Victorian mansion was built in the 1880s and is rumored to be haunted by the ghost of a former servant girl. Her spirit appeared to members of the Davy family in the 1960s. William Davy, his wife Mary, and his father, William Sr., all encountered the girl's apparition in a third floor bedroom. Her spirit, as described by the onlookers, was a dull white light in the shape of a young girl. The scent of bayberry often accompanies the servant girl. There have been numerous, unsuccessful attempts to gain more information regarding the girl through contact with her spirit. However, an examination of the third floor bedroom revealed the door had been broken down sometime in the past.

THE JAMES MARTIN SCHOOL

It was originally a hospital and a nursing school. The mentally insane, as well as the physically disturbed and afflicted, were treated here. It is now an Alternative Middle School, part of the Philadelphia School District, in the Port Richmond neighborhood of the city.

There are sightings of detached, bloody hands and ghostly faces appearing in mirrors. A section of the attic is blocked off from the inside. However, a ghostly face appears in the window in this section. There are three popular stories, or rumors, that circulate about the ghostly face: (1) boys were cutting class and were somehow able to access the blocked off portion of the attic, where they were trapped; (2) during the building's hospital days, one of the mental patients threw himself out of the window during a crazed fit or suicide attempt; (3) there could have been a murder-suicide or a mutual suicide pact among two of the patients.

Whichever story is true, or if something completely different occurred, traumatic death was the result. Whenever a traumatic death occurs, chances for a ghostly sighting increase greatly.

HAUNTED HOUSE on 11TH STREET

This is a residential street. Please be respectful while investigating and photographing.

Many of the ghost stories in this city have been a result (direct or indirect) of the Yellow Fever Epidemic of 1793. What could leave a more traumatic fingerprint than an outbreak of disease? The following account is one of the most tragic stories I have found in my research. Fittingly, I found no exact address nor the identity of the man in this story, but the general location is the east side of 11th Street, between Walnut and Spruce Streets.

Yellow Fever struck the man who lived in the house there in 1793. Believing this man to be dead, his neighbors boarded up the house. In their paranoia, they probably hoped it would keep the disease contained and keep them safe from the spread of infection. The man was not dead. He actually survived the disease, but it left him very weak. In his fragile state, he was able to free a second story window from its boards. Unfortunately, he lost his balance, fell out the window to the sidewalk and died. His back had been broken.

After the epidemic had run its course and the cold weather returned,

Yellow Fever panic faded away. The city eventually returned to its pre-epidemic daily activities. Anguished moans and screams were heard from the vacant property. Sightings of a ghostly face of a man in pain and full of terror in the second story window were also reported.

SUPERNATURAL DATA: church bells

The ringing of church bells was thought to drive away demons. When plagues or epidemics struck cities, the church bells would ring constantly to cleanse the air of the illness. Also, when church bells are heard at sea, it is an omen that someone on the ship will die.

The Bells, Verse V

By Edgar Allan Poe

Hear the tolling of the bells,
*   Iron bells!*
What a world of solemn thought their
*   monody compels!*
In the silence of the night
How we shiver with affright
At the melancholy menace of their tone!
For every sound that floats
For the rust within their throats
*   Is a groan.*
And the people—ah, the people,
They dwell up in the steeple,
*   All alone,*
And who tolling, tolling, tolling,
In that muffled monotone,
Feel a glory in so rolling
On the human heart a stone—
They are neither man nor woman,
They are neither brute nor human,
*   They are Ghouls:*
And their king it is who tolls.

EDGAR ALLAN POE
NATIONAL HISTORIC SITE

7TH AND SPRING GARDEN STREETS

Edgar Allan Poe lived in this house with his young bride/cousin Virginia Clemm and her mother. While in Philadelphia, he worked as an editor for *Burton's Gentleman's Magazine*. In the six years he resided in the City of Brotherly Love, his literary creativity blossomed and flourished. He composed *The Tell Tale Heart*, *The Fall of the House of Usher*, and *Murders in the Rue Morgue*.

When visiting this site, there are no furnishings like in the houses in Society Hill. This is almost a bare empty shell with actual brick and plaster visible. A trip to the basement will send shivers up your spine, as you imagine images of *The Black Cat*.

Edgar Allan Poe was definitely an artist in his composition of the psychological thriller. Perhaps it was because he was such a complex man with a series of tragedies in his life that shaped him in this manner. He had a true gift of looking into the abyss of men's souls and penning the horrible, macabre journey they take. He was fascinated by death and it surrounded him from an early age.

The following poem, *The Sleeper*, is one of my favorite poems of his. He likens death to sleeping, making it seem to be a very soft, frail state, completely the opposite of the permanent, cold existence it really is. We know Edgar Allan Poe is a presence at the Fairmount Waterworks, the now closed General Wayne Inn, his last residence in Baltimore Maryland, and a few other places. However, he may or may not be here as well. If he is in this building, he may be seeking out one of the few times in his life when he was content. Even though this period of contentment was very short lived, it was no doubt memorable to him.

The Sleeper
By Edgar Allan Poe

At midnight, in the month of June,
I stand beneath the mystic moon.
An opiate vapor, dewy, dim,
Exhales from out her golden rim,
And, softly dripping, drop by drop,
Upon the quiet mountain top,
Steal drowsily and musically
Into the universal valley.
The rosemary nods upon the grave;
The lily lolls upon the wave;
Wrapping the fog about its breast,
The ruin moulders into rest;
Looking like Lethe, see! the lake
A conscious slumber seems to take
And would not, for the world, awake.
All beauty sleeps! — and lo! where lies
Irene, with her Destinies!

Oh lady bright! can it be right—
This window open to the night?
The wanton airs, from the tree-top,
Laughingly through the lattice drop—
The bodiless airs, a wizard rout,
Flit through thy chamber in and out,
And wave the curtain canopy
So fitfully—so fearfully—
Above the closed and fringed lid

'Neath which thy slumbering soul lies hid,
That, o'er the floor and down the wall,
Like ghosts the shadows rise and fall!
Oh, lady dear, hast thou no fear?
Why and what art thou dreaming here?
Sure thou art come o'er far-off seas
A wonder to these garden trees!
Strange is thy pallor! strange thy dress!
Strange, above all, thy length of tress,
And this all solemn silentness!

Oh lady sleeps! Oh may her sleep,
Which is enduring, so be deep!
Heaven have her in its sacred keep!
This chamber changed for one more holy,
This bed for one more melancholy,
I pray to God that she may lie
Forever with unopened eye,
With the pale sheeted ghosts go by!

My love, she sleeps! Oh, may her sleep,
As it is lasting, so be deep!
Soft may the worms about her creep!
For in the forest, dim and old,
For her may some tall vault unfold—
Some vault that oft hath flung its black
And winged panels is fluttering back,
Triumphant, o'er the crested palls,
Of her grand family funerals—
Some sepulchre, remote, alone,
Against whose portal she hath thrown,
In childhood, many an idle stone—
Some tomb from out whose sounding door
She ne'er shall force an echo more,
Thrilling to think, poor child of sin!
It was the dead who groaned within.

ALLEN'S LANE

The ghost of a Revolutionary War Soldier galloping down the street with his severed head gripped tightly next to his saddle has been sighted late at night and in the early morning hours. The first encounter dates back to 1775: two British Soldiers witnessed the headless ghost. The most recent sighting was in 1986 by two Philadelphia police officers.

Headless horseman sightings have always fascinated me. This is probably because Washington Irving's *The Legend of Sleepy Hollow* is one of my favorite books. He created this tale in 1820, about a gangly, awkward, gold-digging schoolteacher named Ichabod Crane. He competes with the handsome and athletic Brom Bones for the hand of heiress Katrina von Tassel.

The Headless Horseman was a dead Hessian soldier decapitated by a cannon ball. The horseman chased Ichabod one night, and Ichabod was never seen or heard from again. This story is said to be based on the poem *Tam o' Shanter* by Robert Burns. However, Burns wrote this poem in 1790, fifteen years after the first sighting of the headless ghost of Allen's Lane. Could art or poetry be imitating life? Anything is possible!

Another headless horseman sighting in the area occurred at Paoli National Battlefield. On September 30, 1777, during the Battle of Paoli, a detachment of Continental Soldiers was killed. One of the soldiers was decapitated as a result of the fighting. On September 30th, the anniversary of the day of the battle, the headless soldier rides through the town of Paoli. If you happen to be in Paoli on September 30th and witness this supernatural sight, do your best not to stare at him: it is incredibly rude to do so, but that is not the reason. He may hand you his severed head. Unfortunate for you if he does—the grisly legend states you will be dead within the year.

"If I can but reach the bridge," thought Ichabod, "I am safe." Just then he heard the black steed panting and blowing close behind him; he even fancied that he felt his hot breath…and now Ichabod cast a look behind to see if his pursuer should vanish according to rule, in a flash of fire and brimstone. Just then he saw the goblin rising in his stirrups and in the very act of hurling his head at him. Ichabod endeavored to dodge the horrible missile, but too late. It encountered his cranium with a tremendous crash—he was tumbled headlong into the dust, and Gunpowder, the black steed and the goblin rider, passed by like a whirlwind…an inquiry was set on foot and after diligent investigation they came upon his traces…on the broad part of the brook, where the water ran deep and black, was found the hat of the unfortunate Ichabod, and close beside it a shattered pumpkin…they shook their heads, and came to the conclusion that Ichabod had been carried off by the galloping Hessian."

– Excerpt from The Legend of Sleepy Hollow, *by Washington Irving*

There have been other headless horseman sightings throughout the United States. Here are two of them. Note how the horseman takes on the local characteristics of the area in which he haunts.

In the state of Texas in 1850, a Texas Ranger named Creed Taylor apprehended a rustler/thief named Vidal. He allegedly stole a few of Taylor's mustang ponies. Taylor beheaded Vidal and tied him to the back of a mustang with a sign of warning: the pony was left to wander with the dead man behind it as a message of what would happen to would be thieves or rustlers. Sightings of El Muerto, the headless one, were witnessed by soldiers, travelers, and ranchers until about 1969.

In Santa Fe, New Mexico, sightings of a phantom headless horseman riding from Alto Street to the Santa Fe River have been reported.

GRUMBLETHORPE HISTORIC HOUSE

5267 GERMANTOWN AVENUE

Grumblethorpe mansion is an 18th-century Georgian house, built in 1744 by John Wistar. He was a wealthy wine importer and merchant. It was originally built as John Wistar's summer home, but it eventually became his primary residence.

In the autumn of 1777, British General James Agnew (despite his red coat status, he was known to be a kind and dignified man) was leading his troops up Germantown Avenue. He was shot by a sniper and mortally wounded. Wescott, in *The Historic Mansions of Philadelphia*, reports on the drama of the event:

"The fatal ball entered the small of his back, near the seam of his coat, right side, and came out a little below his left breast...another ball went through his right hand."

General Agnew was immediately taken to John Wistar's home. He died in Grumblethorpe, and as a result of this, General Agnew's blood was imbedded on the parlor floor. Westcott continues:

"General Agnew was taken to the Wistar House, where he died, and stains are still shown on the floor which were from the blood of his wounds."

Now, over 230 years later, the faded stains of the general's blood are clearly visible. Over two centuries of scrubbing and cleaning, etc, cannot remove the blood from the floor. General Agnew has also decided to stay at Grumblethorpe over the years. There have been sightings of his apparition.

Another spirit, a young woman named Justina, also haunts Grumblethorpe. She was orphaned as a result of the Yellow Fever Epidemic of 1793, and the Wistars invited her to live with them. Every Friday evening, Justina baked loaves of bread for the poor. They were distributed on Saturday morning.

In 1820, Justina died, but her spirit remained at Grumblthorpe. According to the Delaware County Ghost Hunters website, Friday evenings after sunset are the best times to encounter Justina's apparition. Sometimes the aroma of fresh baked bread follows her spirit.

In 1826, William Wistar wanted to marry Sarah Logan Fisher (a Quaker woman). Neither of the families approved of the union. However, William's uncle Charles took pity on the couple. He allowed them to be married at Grumblethorpe. Ironically, the wedding nuptials took place in the same parlor as General Agnew's blood.

CLIVEDEN MANSION or CHEW HOUSE

6401 Germantown Avenue

This house was originally owned by Benjamin Chew. Chief Justice Chew also owned another mansion in the city. Wescott from the *Historic Mansions of Philadelphia* says this of the country retreat of Benjamin Chew:

> "Mr. Chew gave the name Cliveden and for some years after it was finished and during provincial times, it was the abode of elegance, hospitality and ease. It was at this venerable house occurred some of the most memorable incidents of the Battle of Germantown."

Chief Justice Chew was a loyalist and allowed British soldiers to hide inside Cliveden, where they fired on General George Washington. As a result, 56 Patriots were killed. The entrance way still has holes in the doorway from musket ball fire.

The legend of the Headless Woman in Cliveden Mansion is a tragic story, in the sense of being an at-the wrong-place-at-the-wrong-time sort of event. She was a resident of Germantown, but her identity remains a mystery. She somehow saw the British troops entering into Germantown. She hid in the basement at Cliveden instead of trying to pass by them or move around them in some way. She was eventually discovered by the British Soldiers. When this happened, one of the soldiers was overtaken by some type of crazed fit and decapitated her. He then ran from the house with her severed head, screaming at the Patriot Soldiers. The true origin of this legend remains unknown.

Benjamin Chew's grand-daughter, Anna Sophia Penn Chew, worked very hard to preserve the estate, even though her brother sold many of the family's heirlooms. People who visit Cliveden report the fragrance of her perfume in the air. Anna Sophia is known to be a welcoming spirit with an extremely positive energy.

LOUDON MANSION

The mansion was built in 1801 in the Federal Style of architecture. Thomas Arnat gave the house its name after Loudon County in Virginia, which was the first place he settled after coming to America from England. The site on which the house was built was from the Battle of Germantown, specifically on top of ground known to have been a burial site for the casualties of war. A wing was added to the house after 1830. Loudon remained in the family until 1939, when Maria Dickinson Logan donated the mansion and its contents to the City of Philadelphia. She also died that same year.

It is believed Loudon is the home of five earthbound spirits/entities. The first is the most recent owner of the mansion, Maria Dickinson Logan. Her ghost has been seen in her old bedroom. Some of her personal items are on display in the house. These items are often moved around. It is almost as if some invisible someone is using a specific item and returning it when finished with it. Maria was not exactly the warm and loving type in life. So, it is not surprising she is the same in her afterlife. She is very resentful of strangers intruding on her privacy. There are also accounts of a woman who was sleeping in Maria's bedroom and witnessed the ghost of an older, bitter woman with a clenched fist sitting on the edge of the bed. If she does not want visitors in Loudon, why in heaven's name did she donate it to the city of Philadelphia? Next, there is a ghost of a little boy named Willie. William Arnat Logan, who was mentally challenged, was believed to be the son of Gustavus and Anna Logan. Willie died in 1860 at the age of 8 years old. Reports and sources all agree Willie is a very mischievous little boy/ghost. He likes to move things around, hides things and very often puts things in places where they do not belong. There is also a shadow man. He was sighted near the staircase. The ghost of a woman in a rocking chair has been witnessed in the sun room. Finally, there is a spirit of a little girl about 6 or 7 years old. She wanders the hallways late at night.

There are also reports from people who have taken photos at Loudon Mansion that their pictures contain orbs and columns of white light.

SUPERNATURAL DATA: orbs

Orbs are thought by many to be the souls of those who crossed over. They can be transparent or solid. Sometimes, they contain an image within themselves, like a deceased person's face or favorite object (piece of jewelry and so on). Orbs, from the perspective of the hard core paranormal investigator, can also be perceived as dust, dirt or something not supernatural at all.

BALEROY MANSION

CHESTNUT HILL
Baleroy mansion is a private residence.
Please be respectful when photographing.

Baleroy was built in 1811, by George Meade Easby, great grandson of the Civil War general George Meade (Battle of Gettysburg, July 1st, 2nd, and 3rd, 1863). This particular house is rumored to be the most haunted house in the city of Philadelphia. Several spirits call Baleroy Mansion home.

Young George Meade Easby was only 6 years old when his family moved into the house. His brother, Stephen, was only 5 years old. As soon as they arrived, the two brothers ran into the courtyard to see their reflections in the water in the fountain. Young George saw his own little face in the water, but Stephen's reflection was not a face at all. It was a bare skull or a skeleton face. The young boy died shortly after that incident.

Even though Stephen passed away, he never really left Baleroy. George Meade Easby was the owner of Baleroy, in residence, until his passing in 2005. He truly believed in the existence of spirits, ghosts, and all things supernatural. His hospitality was well known, as was his gracious and kind nature.

The ghost of Thomas Jefferson has been seen in the formal dining room. Even our third president enjoyed Mr. Meade's hospitality. Another spirit, the apparition of a man in monk's attire, the traditional brown robe, is frequently seen in the bedrooms. Perhaps he is one of Johannes Kelpius' followers? There is also a cantankerous ghost of an old woman, who shakes her cane at Mr. Easby's guests in a threatening manner.

The Blue Room is a very strange and peculiar place indeed! It is also the home of a very malicious entity. Reports of her name are conflicting. Some say Amelia, and some say Amanda. Yet another story, or theory, recognizes two completely different entities in the Blue Room. The most popular theory is that one entity is in charge of a chair and the other entity is responsible for the blue fog and depression. In either case, this particular negative energy is believed to have claimed a specific chair in the Blue Room. Anyone who sits in this chair dies shortly after doing so. The female entity or evil spirit has claimed four victims to date. Amanda is believed to be the cause of the blue fog and depression. Even though she is the most acknowledged of all the spirits in the house, she is not related to George Meade. Her haunting this particular house remains a mystery. She appeared on the staircase to a former curator. The rumor was he sat in her mysterious death chair. After sitting in the deadly chair, he believed he was losing his mind. He died a month to the day after sitting in the infamous chair. A psychic was brought in to analyze the situation and attempt to contact the former curator. Her theory regarding the curator is the opposite of the popular belief. She thinks Amanda helped the curator cross over and that she is not an evil entity. For the record, the former curator has joined the ranks of spirits enjoying their afterlife at Baleroy Mansion!

George Meade's younger brother Stephen haunts Baleroy, too. A few restoration workers saw Stephen in one of the upstairs windows. One of the men saw a small boy with blonde hair. As soon as he called the other workers to view him, the boy vanished before their eyes. Some of the workers refused to return to the house to finish the job after that particular incident.

On yet another day, one of the workers and his son were in the house. The father worked on the 3rd floor and the son was in the basement. The son heard someone calling his name, over and over. The son answered, and received no reply. Only the father was in the house—on the 3rd floor. The son refused to work in the basement after that incident.

George Meade has also encountered other family members, not just Stephen. His uncle and his mother have been seen and heard. They present themselves with loud footsteps, knock on doors, and (very creepily) depress on a bed as if someone is sitting on it, but no one is there.

Finally, one evening, George Meade was entertaining company when he heard a very loud crash. He began a search, only to find the portrait of Stephen was on the floor of the gallery. It had come off the wall and took a 15-foot flight across the room. The nail remained in the wall, and the wire was intact on the back of the portrait. That specific incident still remains a mystery without explanation to this day.

GENERAL WARREN INN

16 Village Way
Malvern, Pennsylvania

The Inn was built in 1745 and originally called the Admiral Vernon Inn. Admiral Vernon was a naval officer who gained popularity as a hero in the French Indian War. The Inn became a Loyalist or Tory gathering place. It was later renamed the General Warren Inn, in an attempt, albeit a small one, to appease the Whigs or Patriots. It was a popular stop on the old turnpike.

The supernatural activity here is across the board. Lights turn on and off all by themselves at any given time. Sightings of a ghost of a blacksmith have been reported. He haunts the third floor. His death was the result of torture and cruelty at the hands of the British Soldiers before the Battle of Paoli. Ghostly voices and phantom growls—disembodied fragments of conversation and growling—are reported throughout the building. A ghost radio, or ghost box, session revealed ghosts of British Soldiers and a woman named Margaret, who said she fell to her death.

GENERAL LAFAYETTE INN

646 Germantown Pike

The Marquis de Lafayette and his men camped around the inn. General George Washington met them there.

There are reports of ghostly historical events and historical counts replaying themselves. Sightings of ghostly women in distress and apparitions of frightened men and women are seen here. A woman was allegedly murdered inside the inn. Also, the ghostly images of father and son caretakers of the property have been seen on the grounds of the inn.

THE HELIBRON MANSION

The ghosts of a distraught mother and murderous farm hand haunt the site of the mansion. The original Helibron Mansion was built in 1837 by

Joseph Edwards. The farm hand, Elisha Culbert, allegedly raped and strangled 14-year-old Margaret Edwards in 1864. The girl's body was found by her mother. She committed suicide shortly after her daughter's death by hanging herself from an upstairs window in the house. A local vigilante mob lynched Culbert from a tree on the property. This incident is the subject of the book *Night Stalks The Mansion* by Constance Westbie and Harold Cameron.

The Helibron Mansion burned down years ago, but there were plans to restore it. It was located west of Ridley Creek in Middleton Township in Delaware County, southwest of the city of Philadelphia.

THE GENERAL WAYNE INN

The Wayside Inn was built in 1704 on land originally owned by William Penn. It has changed owners and names ("Tavern") over the years. The first sale of the tavern resulted in the name change to the Ordinary Tunis. It was under the ownership of Anthony Tunis and the building was used as a mail stop. Benjamin Franklin, postmaster of the colonies, set up an office in there, too.

In May, 1776, Abraham Streeper and his wife, Hannah, purchased the building. Again the name was changed to Streeper's Inn. Soon after buying the tavern, Abraham enlisted in the Continental Army to fight the British. It was at this time the Inn played host to colonial "rock stars." General George Washington, General Anthony Wayne, and the Marquis de Lafayette are among the tavern's most famous and historic visitors.

Hannah Streeper was definitely a Patriot sympathizer. Therefore, the Inn became a fabulous spying locale. Both the British and Hessian soldiers frequented the Inn, drank a little too much, and had a tendency to boast and talk a lot in a drunken state. When the British and Hessians occupied the building, Hannah was put into jeopardy. There was a rumor circulating that the Patriots had dug a tunnel in the basement of the building. It was in that particular location, in the basement tunnel, that the Inn received its first ghost.

Here's the story: a Hessian mercenary went into the basement to get more liquor. He never returned to his party. The Patriot soldiers were hiding in the tunnel and were afraid their hiding spot would be discovered. So, they killed the Hessian and buried the body in the tunnel. No body was discovered (nor any physical evidence), no evidence of a crime committed, and most important, no one discovered the hiding spot of the Patriots.

In 1848, the Inn was used as a polling place on Election Day. One of the workers went into the basement to get more ballots. She saw the apparition of a soldier wearing a green coat. The ghostly soldier faded away. The poll worker thought he was frightened. Hessian Soldiers did wear green jackets during the time of the Revolutionary War. More sightings of the dead soldier in the green jacket have been reported over the years. All witnesses report the same (or very similar) details. He seems scared or frightened by something unknown and then promptly fades away.

The other two possible explanations for this frightened Hessian ghost are as follows: (1) Hannah Streeper allowed a wounded soldier to stay in the basement, where he died of injuries or was killed by Hannah herself; (2) after the Revolution, the Hessians were abandoned by the British soldiers. They feared execution if caught by the patriots. So, a few of them hid in the basement of the Inn which they perceived to be a safe watering hole. One (possibly) developed pneumonia and died in the basement, and the others abandoned him.

Other Revolutionary War ghosts can be spotted at the Inn, some as recent as the 1990s. A seating hostess was preparing an area for dinner service. Someone called her name over and over again. She turned to see who was calling her. It was the ghost of a Revolutionary War Soldier in full uniform, only a few steps away from her. The hostess was shocked. She said he (the ghost) appeared to be solid, unlike a transparent or semi-transparent ghost or apparition.

Also in the 1990s, a maître d' reported this gruesome event. He was in the kitchen when the severed head of a Hessian soldier appeared in a cupboard. The head was looking directly at him. He ran from the kitchen shouting and screaming. This Hessian is believed to be the one that was ambushed and killed by the Patriot soldiers. They beheaded him and disposed of his head and body.

Finally, a British soldier/officer is believed to haunt the building too. He was wounded in battle and brought to the Inn, where he died of complications due to his injuries. He clenched a gold locket tightly in his fist. After he died, the locket was removed from his grip and opened. Inside was a painting of a young woman, obviously the officer's beloved. The soldier was buried without the locket. There have been many ghostly interactions with this soldier over the years. He will appear to someone and demand the locket. When he does not receive the locket, he vanishes into thin air.

There is also a mischievous entity that enjoys the occasional practical joke at the employees' expense. The prankster ghost has moved table settings in the dining rooms, thrown towels in the kitchen, filled glasses stored on the shelves with water, and also filled the ones on the wine rack, too.

The General Wayne has changed hands again and again. In 1987, innkeeper Bart Johnson witnessed some strange events. One evening, after changing many of the light bulbs, he looked up to the lamps only to find they were unscrewing themselves one at a time. He also saw the Hessian soldier in the basement, this time he was only visible from the knees up.

A psychic named Mr. Benio went to the General Wayne. He told the owner he had been having dreams of a Hessian soldier. The soldier told Benio he wanted a proper burial. He begged Benio to go to the Inn. The psychic also reported three ghostly Hessian soldiers. One was named Paul, and the other was named Hans. The third man refused to give his name to Mr. Benio. He also saw the spirit of a young woman from the Revolutionary War Era. She was a maid there, and was raped and killed in the building. She was then buried in the church yard next door. This woman's ghost had revealed herself to the employees before. She was running through the hallway and fighting with an unseen attacker.

The final incarnation of the General Wayne Inn was in 1996. Chefs Jim Webb and Guy Sileo bought the building. It was a major renovation and business project. The restaurant itself needed a lot of TLC, but the chefs believed they were up to the challenge and could restore the General Wayne to its previous glory.

When the restoration and running the restaurant proved to be too much, Sileo began fighting with Webb. The result was a major controversy ending with Chef Sileo being convicted of murdering his partner, Chef Webb, and of committing perjury. After that incident, the General Wayne was sold (again), but this time it was converted into business offices. It is now supposed to be turned into a Jewish synagogue and restaurant. No one knows what lies ahead (and what lies beneath) the General Wayne Inn in terms of its future.

VALLEY FORGE
NATIONAL MILITARY PARK

Valley Forge, Pennsylvania

During the winter of 1777-1778, General George Washington and the Continental Army camped here. This was one of the most brutal, harsh winters known to the state of Pennsylvania. General Washington's men were hungry and poorly clothed. Food provisions had all but dwindled into nothing. The men were ill equipped to deal with the snow and cruel winter. Some were shoeless, while others had insufficient clothing. This was an encampment site only. No battle was fought on this ground, unlike the Battle of Trenton or the Battle of Germantown. It was during this time that General Washington sank into a deep despair, questioning his authority and military knowledge and skill.

At the darkest moments of the Revolution, after General Washington's defeat at New York, followed by the retreat across New Jersey toward Philadelphia, Thomas Paine brought out the first of his *Crisis Papers* (December 1776):

"These are the times that try men's souls. The summer soldier and the sunshine patriot will, in this crisis, shrink from the service of their country; but he that stands it now, deserves the love and thanks of man and woman. Tyranny, like hell, is not easily conquered; yet we have this consolation with us, that the harder the conflict, the more glorious the triumph."

It roused the colonists with his famous words, "these are the times that try men's souls," and with the denunciation of the "summer soldier and sunshine patriot." General Washington had *Crisis 1* read aloud to his soldiers before they crossed the Delaware River to defeat the Hessians in the Battle of Trenton. The *Crisis Papers*, like the Declaration of Independence, was a very angry document. It fed the emotions of rebellion and righteous anger toward oppression. It is the energy of this strong patriotic emotion that has endured over the centuries.

As we have witnessed, instances of Revolutionary Soldier ghosts prove their emotions are just as strong as the ghosts of the unrequited lovers or star-crossed lovers. Many ghostly sightings of spectral figures of soldiers have been reported in the park. There are also reports of disembodied voices and moans of men in agony; probably, the men were overcome with hunger and the fierce winter elements. People have reported seeing ghostly camp fires burning. On stormy (snowy and icy) winter nights, there have been sightings of ghosts walking in the park. Perhaps they are General Washington's dedicated guards not abandoning their posts. Park guides have seen soldiers in uniform, thinking they were re-enactors, only to find that no re-enactors were scheduled on that specific day in the park. Finally, there is a form seen dangling from a tree. When people or tourists get close enough to examine it, they see the shape of a man dangling. They usually run to get help, only to find the dangling man/figure is gone. Stories tell of a spy that was hanged there during the Revolutionary war.

Then there is the vision of the angel who appeared to General Washington. In 1780, George Washington confided in his aide, George Sherman an account of a beautiful apparition or angel who appeared to him at Valley Forge during his time of need. She revealed the future of America to General Washington. This visitation inspired General Washington's Farwell Address. It was in this speech that he warns of a permanent alliance with foreign powers accruing a large public debt, and encourages a "small artful few" to continue or change government.

MOUNT PLEASANT MANSION

Fairmount Park

The mansion was built by Scottish sea captain John Macpherson, as a country estate. There were rumors circulating about Captain Macpherson's double life as a pirate. In 1775, our second president, John Adams, said Mount Pleasant Mansion was the most elegant seat in Pennsylvania. Captain Macpherson was well liked and respected among our Founding Fathers. He unfortunately had one of his arms shot off while at sea.

Apparitions of a man with one arm have been reported throughout the mansion. A security guard reported seeing a pair of red slippers walking down the staircase with no one inside them.

LEMON HILL MANSION

Fairmount Park

In 1799, Henry Pratt purchased the property from Robert Morris. In 1800, Mr. Pratt built the mansion and called it Lemon Hill after the lemon trees in their greenhouses. Visitors report the scent of fresh lemons, even though the greenhouses and trees are long gone from the estate.

There are reported sightings of apparitions of previous gardeners, who are still diligently tending to their gardens. In the 1990s, a police officer (now retired) told two officers on patrol he saw a woman in white. She was walking from the mansion and crossed the road in front of the police cruiser heading in the direction of the Schuykill River. They (the police officers) felt she may be in some kind of trouble. So, they followed her and called out to her, but she did not respond. They continued to follow her, and she disappeared before their eyes.

KING GEORGE II INN

Bristol, Pennsylvania

Bristol is a very lovely historic waterfront town. The King George II is one of the most romantic and picturesque restaurants in the tri-state area. It is also haunted. The basement of the restaurant is said to have been a jail at one time.

Employees will not go down there alone, and they do not relish the thought of going into the basement with each other.

Apparently, some unspeakable acts were committed there in the days that it was a jail. There is a story of a step-sister, who lived in one of the upstairs (residence) rooms. During the time she lived there, she reported hearing a disembodied screaming and sobbing of an infant/baby. The ghostly sobbing came from deep inside the walls.

Finally, a ghost sighting was caught on security film footage—isn't modern technology wonderful? The manager, while reviewing the security films, saw the ghostly apparition of a man dancing. He was dressed in 19th-century period clothing. He was even wearing a top hat! The apparition appeared to be a little drunk and/or tipsy, but, nonetheless, happy and enjoying himself. Although the film itself was a little hazy and grainy, it was obvious to the manager the image was not a living, breathing man. Plus, none of the tenants look like this gentleman, nor do they wear top hats.

MIDNIGHT MARY

BORDENTOWN ROAD, BRISTOL, PENNSYLVANIA

According to the legend, Halloween night is the best time to see Midnight Mary. She does materialize other nights throughout the year, not just on Halloween night. Her legend is a popular one in the realm of the paranormal myth. Other cities in America have their own Midnight Mary myth. She is a beautiful girl, who goes to the prom in a pretty pink dress. She gets a ride home from a handsome young man, who has had too much to drink. Unfortunately, the car ends up in Tullytown lake: both driver and passenger are dead. The boy's body was found, but Mary never came out of the river.

Now, she's a spectral being, wandering on Bordentown Road. Sounds like a cheesy legend or "B" rate Roger Corman movie. However, many people from all walks of life have seen and reported Mary in her pink dress walking on Bordentown Road. A trucker called police after picking up a girl hitchhiking. A puddle was the only thing that remained on his passenger seat after she vanished. A young woman pushing her child in a stroller along the Tullytown River bank saw a figure in pink glide across the water. Many witnesses have reported similar stories to date.

ST JAMES EPISCOPAL CEMETARY

Cedar Street, Bristol Pennsylvania

Inside the St. James Episcopal Cemetery is the grave of a young woman, named Gertrude Spring. She was killed in a car accident in 1935. Many believe she is the source of the Midnight Mary legend.

There is also a Witch's Chair in this cemetery. The location of the chair is next to the grave of Merritt P. Wright and relatively close in proximity to Gertrude Spring's grave. The chair itself is an old wrought iron chair with an absolutely wicked legend, which states, if anyone sits in the iron chair at midnight in the month of October, he/she will be trapped in the embrace of the witch.

(Let me state, for the record, I did drive up and down Bordentown Road in the hopes of seeing Midnight Mary. Unfortunately for me, it was an unproductive trip. However, I doubt I will ever be brave/crazy enough to sit in that iron chair at midnight in the month of October.)

MARGARET GRUNDY MEMORIAL LIBRARY

Radcliffe Street, Bristol, Pennsylvania

In the 1800s, the Keene Mansion stood on the grounds of the Library. Sarah Keene was beautiful and many young men aspired to be her husband. One of her would be suitors was none other than Joseph Bonaparte—remember him?—brother of Napoleon, exiled King of Spain and Naples, brief resident of 9th Street in center city Philadelphia (Bonaparte House). He traveled by row boat to the Keene Mansion to court beautiful Sarah Keene. Unfortunately, she was not as into him as he was into her.

It seems ironic that the ghost of Chloris (a victim of unrequited love) haunts the Bonaparte house and grounds, and Joseph Bonaparte's fate is also to be a victim of unrequited love. It is also his anguished love-starved ghost that haunts this area. His apparition carries a lantern and travels the path to the Delaware River. He seems to be making a valiant attempt to court beautiful Sarah Keene in death, also.

BOLTON MANSION

HOLLY HILL, LEVITTOWN, PENNSYLVANIA

This was the second house in America built by Phineas Pemberton in 1790. Pemberton was a friend of William Penn and his first house was built on the land next to Penn's acreage. Pemberton's first house, however, was built on wetlands. His first wife, his parents, and some of his children died, and Pemberton blamed their deaths on the wetlands.

So, he built a new home. He eventually married again to Anne Harrison, and named his new home Bolton after his childhood home in England. Bolton was passed on to the Morris family (through marriage). Before the Civil War, tunnels were dug and James Morris used the mansion as a stop on the Underground Railroad. The Morrises were wealthy upper class people. James was furious when his daughter, Mary, wanted to marry a man of lower social status. She was forbidden to see him. (Does this story sound familiar? Perhaps a Philadelphia ghost legacy is forbidden love between social classes and the tragic deaths that result from the star-crossed lovers.)

However, she was madly in love, and waited anxiously for his return, but he never returned to her. In despair and desperation, Mary hanged herself on the main staircase. The background of Mary's lover remains a mystery. Some say he was a soldier and died in battle. Some say he was financially compensated (James Morris allegedly gave him big bucks) to leave Mary. No one really knows for sure. Another suicide took place at Bolton years after Mary's tragic death. A manservant also committed suicide by hanging himself, by tying off a rope and jumping from the second story window. The reason for his suicide is unknown.

Mary's story is the one that sparks the most response for sightings. In 1938, students from Penn State were allowed to raise crops and livestock on the grounds of Bolton Mansion. They also reported seeing the ghost of a young woman walking down the stairs and sometimes hanging from the stairs. Others sighted a man hanging from the side of the house. A ghostly little girl was seen looking out of the same window. They also reported disembodied voices and black shadows in the basement.

The house often changed ownership—U.S. Steel, William Levitt, and Bristol Township, to name a few. It was finally abandoned and scheduled for the wrecking ball. The Friends of the Bolton Mansion saved it and hoped to restore it to its former glory, even though it was a time consuming job.

Since the restoration has begun, several sightings have occurred. Neighbors reported seeing a woman in a long dress and cloak walking around the property at night. They know she is an apparition because she glows in the dark. Another apparition, also a woman, is seen on the property as well. She cries and frantically searches for something—maybe her child?

The basement of the house is also active. The ghost of a woman appears at the fireplace, maybe cooking, before fading away. The other section of the basement is where the Underground Railroad tunnels are located. A ghostly little girl is seen here at the entrance to the tunnels. She is singing and not affected by human viewers. Finally, an investigative group was brought in to evaluate. They reported the basement was very active with the spirit of a child. She touched one of the investigators and grabbed another investigator's shirt.

PEN RYN MANSION

BENSALEM, PENNSYLVANIA

The mansion was built in 1744 by Abraham Bickley, a very wealthy shipping entrepreneur. The estate consists of 100 acres of gardens and lawns that lead to the banks of the Delaware River. Additions to the mansion property itself came later, in the 1890s, under the direction and scrutiny of Lucy Wharton Drexel. She added a carriage house, servants' quarters, an art gallery, and a library in the duration of time in which she owned the property. It remained a private residence and was then converted into a school. Later, from 1988 to 1993, the mansion was abandoned.

Fortunately, Pen Ryn Mansion was placed on the National Register of Historic Places and was restored and converted to an upscale banquet facility. Mr. Bill Haas is the proprietor of the mansion and very familiar with its legends and folklore. According to Mr. Haas, Pen Ryn has its very own Christmas Ghost.

Abraham Bickley and his family were Tory sympathizers. Because of Bickley's wealth and fortune, he was able to fund the British soldiers in the Revolution against the Patriot Soldiers. Abraham had seven children, all of whom lived and died at Pen Ryn. All seven of his children also remained unmarried, something highly unusual during that time (and a little creepy too).

Robert Bickley, son of Abraham, had intentions of marrying one of the colonists. He brought his Patriot fiancé to Pen Ryn to meet his family on Christmas Eve. Needless to say, Abraham not only disapproved of his future daughter-in-law, he was infuriated with his son in choosing her. After a heated argument, Robert stormed out of the house rather dramatically, and (stupidly) threw himself into the icy water of the Delaware River. The Delaware can be most unforgiving on a summer day, but on a freezing December night, it can only be deadly. Needless to say, Robert never returned to Pen Ryn—alive, anyway. Abraham was troubled over the fight, but believed his son would return home once his anger dissipated and he settled down.

Later that evening, there was a loud knock at the front door. Upon opening it, there were no physical signs of Robert or anyone else. Abraham was confused. Apparently this event replays itself over and over again, and on other occasions besides Christmas Eve night. The facts is always the same. First, a loud knocking or rapping is heard at the front door. When someone answers the door, there is no physical person there. Some reports mention disembodied moaning and other noises. Sometimes a misty apparition of a man will appear, soaking wet and wearing a tattered cloak. He then disappears into thin air. Robert (supposedly) loyally appears every Christmas Eve night at Pen Ryn Mansion. Some specially devoted people honor Robert, who died for love, with a vigil in the mansion every Christmas Eve.

THE TEMPERANCE HOUSE

NEWTOWN (LOCATED IN THE HISTORIC DISTRICT), PENNSYLVANIA

The Temperance House was established in 1772 by owners Andrew and Nancy McGinn. They provided a combination school for children and a tavern for adults (a gathering place). The Inn grew and served clientele from all walks of life in the surrounding area, from common laborers to Continental Army officers.

In 1835, Constable Chillion W. Higgs took the temperance part of the name way too seriously and prohibited the sale of liquor at the Temperance House. It remained a soft drink institution for 130 years. In 1963, H. Clifton Neff bought the Temperance House and the imposed prohibition was lifted. Spirits were served again, and sometimes spirits are served to spirits!

There are two ghosts who have taken up residence at the Temperance House. They are very endearing ghosts, too. There are two ghosts: a boy and a girl, both from the Colonial Era at the tavern. Sightings of the children were very strong and frequent during the time of the restoration. Normally, they run and play in the hallway, like kids from any era. However, there was one unexplained instance: a couple on their honeymoon had a visit from the children. The children seem to prefer four particular rooms at the Inn. The couple happened to be occupying one of those particular rooms. The children ran through the room in the middle of the night.

Sometimes their laughter is heard while they play. The handyman had his own special encounter with one of the children. He was called to do some repair work on one of the rooms. When he opened the door, he was faced with the image of the apparition of the little girl jumping on the bed. He told the little girl that the nice housekeeper had just finished making the bed. She had to stop jumping on it or she would get in trouble. The ghost vanished. The housekeeper has seen the same window open and close all by itself three times. She believes the energy is protective and positive. She believes the children watch over her.

CAPTAIN KIDD'S TREASURE
IN BUCKS COUNTY

The thought of buried pirate treasure in Bucks County seemed impossible to me. I am still searching for complete, tangible proof of pirate activity in Philadelphia, especially that Blackbeard's boots were actually on Philadelphia soil. However, there is actual data that supports a link between Captain William Kidd and Bucks County.

Bowman's tower is an observatory that was built on the site of a Continental Army lookout post. The tower and surrounding hill were named for John Bowman. In 1696, he was the ship's surgeon in a fleet commanded by none other than Captain William Kidd. This fleet was commissioned by the English government to pursue and eliminate the pirate activity on the "seven seas." At that time, pirates were terrorizing and robbing ships. As the legend goes, Captain Kidd turned pirate himself and buried treasure he "liberated" from various other ships on the seas. Captain Kidd was executed in 1700, and his crew was disbanded in New York.

Surgeon John Bowman moved to Newtown, Bucks County. His past eventually caught up to him. Rumors circulated that Bowman brought some treasure with him to Bucks County. The rumors still remain just that: rumors. Surgeon John Bowman is buried on the eastern side of the hill. Another, spookier legend is associated with his final resting place. It is believed that if you kneel at Bowman's grave and repeat the question, John Bowman, what killed you? surgeon Bowman's disembodied voice will answer you, NOTHING!

Another account of the Bowman's treasure legend comes from Dr. J.E. Scott. He wrote the *Historical Account Of Bowman's Hill*. In this account, Scott provides a logical theory regarding John Bowman's buried treasure legend. It is most likely Bowman was sent as a surgeon in the fleet sent to capture Captain William Kidd. Like Kidd, Bowman turned pirate and joined Kidd. He participated in the seizure of Boston and sailed with the crew to Delaware. It was there in Delaware that he parted company with his pirate friends. He then traveled up the Delaware River to Bucks County where he spent his remaining years. He was buried at the summit of the hill. Treasure hunters and treasure seekers assume John Bowman buried some type of treasure before his death.

THE CHURCH OF ST LUKE

HIGHWAY 291, EDDYSTONE, PENNSYLVANIA

This occurrence is mystifying on many levels (and it's a little scary, too). In 1975, a statue of Jesus was located 12 feet above the altar in the church. For a year, from 1975 to 1976, it bled (human blood) from the holes in the palms of its hands. The statue of Jesus was only twenty-eight (28) inches in height. It was X-rayed, and the arms of the statue were broken off to be examined. No signs of foul play or movie-like special effects (tubes or gel packs of fake blood) were detected. The liquid was real human blood (it was tested). This blood poured from the wounds of the hands of the statue, and priests and physicians testified to the authenticity of this paranormal (even holy) phenomenon.

Here's where the story gets really strange. Mrs. Ann Poore was the owner of the statue. A year after the bleeding statue incident, Mrs. Poore began bleeding from wounds in the palms of her hands. The wounds appeared to be bleeding stigmata wounds.

LAMB TAVERN

865 WEST SPRINGFIELD ROAD
SPRINGFIELD, PENNSYLVANIA

The Lamb Tavern has been a landmark in Springfield since 1808. Eamor Eachus originally named the tavern the Three Tuns, and it became a popular watering hole with the locals. In 1835, the name was changed to the Lamb Tavern. In 1881, the owner of the tavern, Malachi Sloan, died. Strangely, he had a clause in his will stating that the Lamb Tavern was no longer able to operate as a hotel. Well, that clause was honored for about 14 years.

In 1895, the Lamb Tavern was back in business. Since then, a Shadow Figure has been seen and reported moving across the hallway. There are also reports of disembodied moans.

TRUM TAVERN

The Trum Tavern is located in Bucks County in the town of Trumbauersville. Elisha Parker owned and operated the Tavern in 1752. It was also used as a meeting house; town meetings were held here. In addition to this, it was a lodge for travelers and a stop for the stage coach. Trum Tavern is, of course, also haunted.

The ghost that haunts Trum Tavern is believed to be Jacob Fries, a colonist. As it turns out, Trum Tavern was called Jacob Fries Tavern, and sometime after, it was called Jakes. According to an upstairs resident Jacob Fries is a most active presence there. She frequently feels his presence while in her residence on the second floor. He occasionally follows her. Having a ghost in residence does not bother her at all, and Jacob is a benevolent spirit.

His ghost has been reported as an old man, dressed in black, with grey hair. Sometimes, he just makes a lot of noise in the upstairs area. Other workers in the Tavern have also been exposed to Jacob's ghost. Some have also seen his ghost. Another former worker believes Jacob enjoys playing with the circuit breakers in the bar. One evening in particular, Jacob shut all but one of the circuit breakers off. Most of the employees believe Jacob's energy is the strongest on the second floor and on the staircase.

CHAPTER V

HAUNTED NEW HOPE

New Hope, Pennsylvania, has been called one of the most haunted towns in the state. This title is understandable because New Hope is also one of the most picturesque towns in Pennsylvania. Located right on the banks of the Delaware River, it is an eclectic, artistic town with theaters, bed and breakfasts, art galleries, and shops. The town of New Hope itself has industrial roots, and was once comprised of mills and tavern houses, businesses reliant upon the canal and Delaware River. The majority of the ghosts that inhabit New Hope are from that Industrial Era, when life was a little rougher than it is today.

THE PINEAPPLE HILL
BED and BREAKFAST

1324 River Road
New Hope, pennsylvania

The Bed and Breakfast is located on River Road, between the towns of New Hope and Washington's Crossing, Pennsylvania.

The Pineapple Inn Bed and Breakfast is an 18th-century country manor house on six acres. The owners believe there are two active spirits at the Bed and Breakfast. One of the ghosts is believed to be John Scott. Mr. Scott was the owner of the Pineapple Hill during the early 1800s. The ghost frequents the oldest part of the manor house, where Mr. Scott resided while living. However his apparition has been witnessed in the other parts of the bed and breakfast, too.

Apparently, Mr. Scott's ghost is very active and affectionate at night. According to the present owners, Mr. Scott's ghost sneaks up the back stairs to the second floor. Sometimes, Mr. Scott's ghost stands over the bed while unsuspecting visitors are sleeping. Sometimes, he even kisses the sleeping patron on the cheek! Talk about an overzealous and over-amorous innkeeper! Lights are always turning on and off by themselves in all areas of the bed and breakfast. Objects move themselves and unexplainable breezes have occurred.

Another strange account from the owners speaks of multiple bed and breakfast guests reportedly having the same dream. That is a very peculiar incident! The guests are not technically related—except in the sense that they experience the same vision during sleep. The dream is as follows: a man is dressed in a black coat with gold buttons, black riding boots, and rides a horse. He is riding on a tree lined street/road. The horse stops suddenly and bucks; the rider tries to get control over the situation. All of the dreamers awoke, never knowing the fate of the horse and the rider.

THE LOGAN INN

10 West Ferry Street
New Hope, pennsylvania

The Logan Inn was established in 1827 as an extension of the Ferry Tavern, which accommodated passengers who traveled the Delaware River from the town of Lambertville, New Jersey. John Wells established the Logan Inn as a resting point along the Old York Road corridor. There was also a livery stable for the horses to be kept there, too. The Inn was named after both James Logan, William Penn's personal secretary, and a Lenape/Lenapi Chief.

Chief Wingahocking spent a great deal of time with James Logan, and respected and loved him. So, the Chief traded names with Mr. Logan. This act of trading names was only reserved for those who were highly respected by the Lenape/Lenapi tribe. So, Chief Wingahocking became Chief Logan and James Logan became Wingahocking. James Logan named a creek after Chief Wingahocking and had a 10-foot metal statue in the Chief's likeness placed on the property. It then became the Logan Inn, in honor of both men.

George Washington was rumored to have stayed here at least five times. Aaron Burr stayed here after his duel with Alexander Hamilton. The Logan Inn also played host to such personalities as Oscar Hammerstein II, the Marx Brothers, and most impressively, Dorothy Parker—one of my favorite writers—and the other writers of the Round Table of the Algonquin Hotel. As the town of New Hope grew and became more and more artistically centered, the Logan Inn kept up with the changing times. It was renovated in 1987. It is also listed on the Register of National Historic Places.

The Logan Inn has a very colorful supernatural history, too. Aaron Burr never really vacated the inn. According to both psychics and mediums, his spirit moves about the inn. Some guests have witnessed a Revolutionary War soldier in full uniform walking from the kitchen to the tavern. Shadow figures have also been reported. They glide through walls and windows. There is even one account of the fireplace coming to a full burning fire all on its own without any assistance, any human assistance that is.

Room Six has the most tales to be told. First, it is the coldest room in the inn, but, logistically speaking, it should not be. People have been tapped on the shoulder in this room. No one (no living human being) was in the room or in close proximity to do the shoulder tapping. A man who was staying in Room Six was awakened in the middle of the night. Someone had opened the door to the room. That particular door was double locked by the man himself. He looked in the hallway and no one was there. Another woman who stayed in Room Six had a pillow pulled from under her head in the middle of the night.

The silhouette of a woman standing outside the door to Room Six has been reported by many guests. The aroma of lavender has also been reported in Room Six, but no plants or sachets have been found in the room to prove the fragrance. A popular belief is that the spirit in Room Six is that of Emily Reiter Lutz, the daughter-in-law of the Lutzes and mother of the innkeeper. Emily passed away at the Inn.

Historically, soldiers would march from Valley Forge to New Hope and stay at the Logan Inn. There were many Revolutionary War soldier deaths, of course. Bodies were stored in the kitchen and basement of the inn because the ground was too frozen to bury them. Those bodies were buried when the ground thawed. There is a ghost of a Revolutionary War soldier in the basement, believed to be one of those soldiers who were there in cold storage.

On the grounds of the Logan Inn, in the year 1946, the annual street fair was held in the parking lot. A palm reader (Parker Dehm) and his customers heard loud, uncontrollable screaming and weeping. It sounded like a child crying. No children were in the immediate area. Dehm closed his tent and went for a (well-deserved) drink. It was Thursday evening, the first day of the fair. The same exact thing happened on the following day, Friday. The sobbing stopped when the fair closed. The following year Dehm set up in the same spot. The screaming began again. By Saturday, crowds had formed to find the sobbing child. No child was found. Dehm left. Participants in fairs that followed avoid that specific spot in the parking lot.

ODETTE'S

1111 RIVER ROAD
NEW HOPE, PENNSYLVANIA

The earliest version of Odette's was definitely not a five-star institution. It was, however, practical, and it served the citizens of Colonial Pennsylvania. The first tavern was built in 1794 at the crest of the Wells Falls rapids. In the early 19th century, the River House served the untamed men who worked on the river.

Then, the building and town fell onto hard economic times. Both New Hope and the River House lived to see an economic rebirth in the 1930s, and during this time, the River House became the first tourist hotel in town.

Famed French actress Odette Myrtil retired from her stage and film career to convert the hotel into a fine dining French restaurant called Chez Odette in 1961. Odette passed away in 1978, and there is no solid evidence that she has remained as a "permanent restaurateur." There is evidence that other ghosts have taken up residence here, though.

The management and staff have witnessed supernatural activity in the restaurant. While the identity of the entities remains a mystery, there seem to be a few different entities in Odette's. According to one of the staff, there is a presence that is on the third floor. Its energy does not seem to be positive, but is suspected to be a ghost from the early days of the River House. Disembodied voices are also plentiful here. At any given time, one of the staff will be working when a man's voice will call his/her name. No one is ever in close proximity to the staff worker to be heard.

Then there is Mimi. She is the ghost of a woman believed to have been murdered in the back bar. These days, Mimi prefers to occupy a booth in that area, and she does not like the living to occupy it. She slams the back door whenever patrons are seated at her table. Finally, a staff member recalls seeing shadows walking past a mirror at the same time she was looking into it.

PARRY MANSION

45 SOUTH MAIN STREET
NEW HOPE, PENNSYLVANIA

Benjamin Parry was one of the wealthiest citizens of the town of New Hope. Parry himself is credited for giving the town its name. He built the mansion in 1784 and resided there with his family for 55 years. Five generations of Parrys were raised in the mansion. Benjamin's grandson, Richard, owned mills on both sides of the Delaware River. In 1966, Margaret Parry Lang sold the mansion to the New Hope Preservation Society, who fully restored the mansion to its former glory. The New Hope Preservation Society has an office located inside the Parry Mansion. They are fully aware of the paranormal activity that occurs inside the house. Various members of the Parry family make themselves known to the members of the New Hope Preservation Society from time to time. This is not surprising because many of the family's personal belongings are on display at the mansion.

Sightings of ghostly children are abundant at the mansion. This is not surprising. Benjamin's oldest son, Oliver, had 12 children and only 8 of them survived. Some of the ghostly children died as children, while some of them simply choose to appear in their childhood form(s). Audio recordings always reveal their footsteps. They laugh out loud, run through the hallways, and act like kids at play. Basically, their mischief is continuing in death.

There is one disturbing account of a small girl in the Victorian Bedroom. She was ill, and the illness drove her mad. Her sickly, fragile little ghostly form is often seen restrained (tied to the bed) and crying. There is also the ghost of a woman in black in the Victorian Bedroom, and some apparitions float freely throughout the house. One in particular is a woman in a black-beaded dress. She floats in various locations in the upstairs.

THE MILL HOUSE

63 FERRY STREET
NEW HOPE, PENNSYLVANIA

The following story, or account, is very creepy not only in a supernatural way, but in a CSI way, as well. When the mill was in business, in full production, this was a foreman's house. This foreman was a widower with a daughter who fell madly in love with a mill worker. The two lovers met in secret, unbeknownst to her father. She became pregnant as a result. Then, the young woman suddenly disappeared without a trace. No one ever saw her again. The young man waited and waited and waited in vain for his lover to contact him.

One night, the neighbors of the foreman heard a great deal of screaming coming from the foreman's home. The neighbors found this puzzling and frightening. No one was aware of the young woman's condition. The screams suddenly stopped as mysteriously as they began. The following day, the foreman and his daughter were gone. Whether the young man knew of his pending fatherhood status remains a mystery.

In the 1960s, the back field of the property was excavated. The remains of a new born baby were found. On cold winter evenings, people from the surrounding area of the property have heard crying of both a girl and a new baby. Some of the residents have even seen the glowing figure of a girl in the area behind the house: another case of the energy of the star-crossed lover returning from the dead, this time in her glowing apparition.

THE INN AT PHILLIPS MILL

2950 RIVER ROAD
NEW HOPE, PENNSYLVANIA

The Inn at Phillips Mill was built in 1756 by Aaron Phillips and was originally a stone barn. The structure was reinvented as an estate house with gardens, and so on. It is on the National Registry of Historic Places, which means the structure of the house, grounds, etc., are protected and must be maintained in its original state (an 18th-century farmhouse).

During the restoration period, spectral energies were attracted to the inn, which is standard operating procedure among the dead. The previous owner of the Inn at Phillips Mill has returned to the home he loved and lived in with his family. Perhaps he decided to stay at the inn, too. There were instances of disembodied footsteps and cold spots. There is also the ghost of a woman in Victorian Era clothing. She seems very interesting because she has made wardrobe changes. Sometimes, she appears in a long gown with a high Victorian collar and, sometimes, she wears a long black skirt with a traditional high-neck white blouse and boots. She haunts the staircase and upstairs hall. She seems to be completely absorbed with her own situation. It is very possible that she is too involved with her own agenda to communicate with any of the living humans at the Inn.

However, she does like to make her presence known by brushing past people on the stairs as they ascend and descend. Those who have experienced this phenomena find it very unnerving for obvious reasons. She has also been reported relaxing in a rocking chair. Some of the wait staff has reported seeing a ghostly dog. The small white canine apparition has been sighted in the hallway and on the back staircase.

THE VAN SANT BRIDGE

NEW HOPE, PENNSYLVANIA

This bridge has a very threatening and imposing history: no wonder it is haunted. Documented ghostly activity associated with the Van Sant Bridge dates back to 1869, with the report of a young man being pursued by a yellow fog or mist-type entity. It followed the young man from the woods into the bridge. A young woman who was pregnant and without a husband was thrown out of her parents' house, faced with the fate of living on the streets with an illegitimate child. The father of her unborn child abandoned her, too. She was desperate and frightened. Overcome with depression, she threw herself off the Van Sant Bridge with her baby in her arms. The haunted legend of the bridge is, if you stand on the bridge and remain very still and quiet, you will be able to hear the baby crying.

Horse thieves were also hanged from this bridge. They often make their ghostly apparitions visible to people in close proximity to the bridge. They are seen as the ghosts of men hanging (swinging) from the rafters of the bridge. There are also reports of a Shadow Figure that glides through the bridge.

THE BLACK BASS HOTEL

3774 River Road
Lumberville, Pennsylvania

The Black Bass Hotel is located six miles north of New Hope along the Delaware River, directly across the river from Bulls Island, New Jersey. The hotel itself is a very British institution: 70% of it has been restored to its former colonial glory. During the time of the Revolution, the Delaware River was a major source of revenue, carrying food and supplies via the waterway.

Tory Loyalists built the Black Bass Hotel in 1745, and the subsequent owners added rooms to the hotel to accommodate the canal and river workers. This is a most extraordinary building. It has survived floods in the 1740s and a fire in 1831, not to mention the Revolutionary War. It was in jeopardy because of its allegiance to the Tory Party and the Crown of England. In 1949, Herbert Ward bought the Hotel, constructed a kitchen, and renovated it to become an upscale suburban hotel. It was auctioned in 2008, and it is now listed as a Historic Place by the United States Department of the Interior.

In terms of the supernatural, this place rocks. There are a few entities that call the Black Bass Hotel home. In the 1830s, a man was killed in a bar fight in the main tavern, which is now called the Lantern Room. The common thought is that the man is either a local citizen or the previous owner of the hotel. He is now a permanent resident of the Lantern Room. There is also a female entity, a rather voluptuous woman (or portly depending on whom is telling the story). She is described as carrying a pearl-handled pistol and is also believed to be a previous owner of the Hotel. She is reported to patrol the hotel (while carrying her gun) and is especially fond of the Grover Cleveland Room. She is sometimes seen on the bed!

Another male ghost makes his presence known in the Lantern Taproom. It is believed he was also the victim of murder. His appearance is reported as "lifeless and grey." He wears velvet-knee pants and a large, wide-brimmed hat with a plume. The apparition of an older woman is also reported in the Lantern Taproom. The popular belief is that she appears to be looking for someone or something. She wanders around and sometimes cries. As we know, renovations made to the property always bring out the dead.

The popular belief is that the Black Bass Hotel is haunted and will remain haunted. This is because the spirits who reside here are willing to make themselves known to the living guests. The dead residents are very protective of the property and want to be sure the living guests respect it.

Appendix I
Exercises & Techniques

MEDITATION TECHNIQUE

The following meditation technique will prepare you for an evening of ghost hunting, spiritual encounters, or any kind of paranormal and/or supernatural experience you anticipate. It is very important to prepare your body, mind, spirit, and energy force for this activity. I recommend burning (or smudging) some sage prior to meditation, and cleansing any instruments you may be using (e.g., a pendulum, camera, etc.) and your protective amulet/talisman in the smoke of the sage. I always cleanse before and after spirit activity. Cleansing after spirit activity is commonly called grounding. This ensures a protective atmosphere and the removal of residual energy. This technique is wonderfully multi-purpose. It can be used whenever you feel run down and need an energy boost or even if you feel too energized and need to wind down and relax. Whatever the purpose, you just visualize what you want. The beauty of meditation really does lie in its simplicity and effectiveness.

LET'S BEGIN.

Sit with your spine straight, either in a chair or crossed legged position on the floor with the palms of your hands resting on your knees. If you are not comfortable with either of those positions, you can lie flat on your back with arms resting by your sides. You do run the risk of falling asleep in this position. So, I usually reserve it for just that—a nighttime right-before-I-sleep meditation. However, you need to do whatever is best for you.

Close your eyes. Take a deep, cleansing breath and feel yourself sinking into complete relaxation. Take two more deep breaths. Picture all the tension leaving your body as you exhale. Inhale the pure glow of relaxation and exhale the polluted smog of stress and tension.

Take another deep, cleansing breath. Picture a glowing white light surrounding your head, like a halo. Breathe at a calm, relaxed pace. The halo is now surrounding your entire body. It is a protective light, keeping you safe and secure. Tension, stress and negativity cannot penetrate this light shield. Peace, love, and happiness are here in this body halo. Feel these positive energies as they surround you.

NOW WE ARE GOING TO COUNT BACKWARDS FROM 5 TO 1, BREATHING DEEPLY AFTER EACH COUNT.

FIVE – Feel all tension completely dissolving. It no longer exists in your body or your world.

FOUR – The white light that surrounds you connects you to all the peace in the universe.

THREE – Feel yourself opening up to the universe; feel the peace, love, and happiness.

TWO – You are becoming one with the universal energy of peace and love.

ONE – You are completely connected to the universe and all of its souls.

Stay here in this peaceful place for a few breaths, soaking in the universal energy of happiness.

WHEN YOU ARE READY, YOU CAN BEGIN COUNTING FORWARD FROM 1 TO 5, BREATHING DEEPLY AFTER EACH COUNT.

ONE – The white light that surrounds you protects and energizes you.

TWO – Feel that energy beginning to grow.

THREE – Feel yourself becoming rejuvenated with the positive energy of the universe.

FOUR – You are open to all positive encounters.

FIVE – You are protected by the energy and light of the universe; it energizes and revitalizes you.

Now, take one final deep, deep (feel it throughout your entire body) breath. Open your eyes. Exhale slowly. You are ready for your spiritual encounters.

GROUNDING EXERCISES

Grounding is a process of contact—connecting with the earth, with its edges, boundaries, and limitations. We are becoming present in the here and now, not floating around. We are solid. Without grounding, we are unstable and lose our center, attention wanders, and we may appear to be "not all here." Basically, it is because we are not. Ground is familiar, safe and secure, with a power all unto itself.

You can perform a specific grounding ritual (cleansing bath, meditation, etc.) or you can make contact with the earth and visualize. Both can be equally effective. It truly is a matter of preference. I have a series of grounding exercises I perform. Sometimes I do all of them, sometimes one or two. I always burn sage sticks and cleanse my amulet/talisman and other items. Sometimes, I touch a tree or grass and picture all residual energy leaving my body.

Again, it is all a matter of what feels comfortable to you—that is the best grounding exercise for you. The following grounding exercises can be performed after spiritual encounters. You can perform just one or a combination. Any one of these can be done as an emergency grounding if you feel surrounded by threatening or negative energies, or if you are just a little out of balance.

STOMPING

This is an excellent way to make contact with the solid earth and an excellent quick fix if you are feeling light headed or threatened. Just stomp each foot several times, while envisioning the protective white light surrounding you. Visualize the dark negative energy being crushed beneath your foot. Feel positive energy replacing the negativity.

JUMPING UP AND DOWN

In doing this, you are making contact with the earth (the solidity and permanence of the earth). You do this by pushing against and sinking in it. It is most effective when performed on grass or dirt, not cement. Be kind to your knees and feet! Again, proper visualization techniques should be done in conjunction with the jumping portion of the exercise. You can visualize a protective white light and/or the removal of negative energy—whatever you feel necessary for this exercise.

MASSAGE

Of course, as a massage therapist and energy worker, I am a huge advocate of foot and leg massage to ground your energy and circulate the blood in your body. I strongly suggest you perform some deep breathing exercises while your legs and feet are being massaged. This will release all residual energy and center you.

EATING

Yes, eating. Many people eat to ground themselves. (Think of Keanu Reeves in the film Constantine.) Eating is an excellent and effective technique, especially after an intense paranormal experience or an emotionally draining spiritual encounter. Either may leave you feeling a little dizzy or light headed. In either case, avoid caffeine and hydrate properly. Most importantly, do not over eat. This will actually make you more imbalanced. Eat balanced and in moderation. Visualize the food balancing you by replacing the feelings of imbalance with a centering and stabilizing feeling.

BATHING/SHOWERING

This is another excellent grounding technique because, as you shower, you can actually visualize all the negative energy going down the drain. This is definitely part of my grounding routine. Not only do you feel revitalized and rejuvenated, but you smell nice, too. It is also a great prelude to meditation and sleep.

SLEEPING

This is the one total, complete grounding exercise that is effective for centering, rest, and rejuvenation. Again, you can employ visualization techniques while you drift off to sleep. Picture yourself free from all residual negative energy, whole, balanced, and revitalized.

Always remember to ground yourself and close all channels after working with spiritual energies, especially when working with a pendulum or spirit board. Cleanse all of your spirit tools, too. Also, perform grounding exercises after doing any type of ghost hunting, whether successful or unsuccessful in your endeavors. This is so important. Failure to do this could result in an imbalance or exhaustion. In extreme cases, a spirit could even follow you or you may be the victim of a psychic attack (symptoms of a psychic attack follow). It is very important to take the proper precautions whenever working with the spirit world.

SYMPTOMS OF A PSYCHIC ATTACK

First, and most important, all things we perceive as bad—occurrences, accidents, coincidences, and so on—are not the result of psychic attacks. We are not under a constant threat of attack from some unseen world or another plane of existence. Life does not imitate horror movies. That said, psychic attacks do occur, and there is a wide variety of symptoms.

A psychic attack, by definition, is the occurrence of dark and negative forces (or energies) originating with a person, location, or an object that attach itself to an individual. These negative energies create a disturbance within the energy of that person. This can be caused by a spirit or energy. This is why grounding is so important. Grounding cleanses our energy fields and protects us from any residual negative energy from clinging on to us. As you will see, symptoms can range from a feeling of envy or jealousy to a headache or sore muscle to something more serious like paranoia and hearing voices (in extreme cases only).

This has happened to everyone at one time or another. It can be the result of improper grounding or not enough grounding. Other factors that can contribute to this may include being stressed over other aspects in life like jobs, health, and so on. It can be compared to the physical manner in which you catch a cold. If you are exposed to the rhinovirus and are run down because of lack of sleep or stress, chances are you will catch a cold. The same principle applies here. If your aura or energy field is compromised because of stress or any other factors, you may experience a psychic "cling-on" of negative energy. The negative energies move freely into and circulate around an individual's energy field or aura (if not properly grounded and cleansed) and into the individual's physical body, too. They may influence what the individual will think. He or she may seem confused, or display negative emotions like jealousy, spite, or envy. Headaches, sore and tired muscles, exhaustion, lack of sleep, and nightmares often occur. A passive person may become aggressive and angry for no reason.

These symptoms can occur because of organic reasons or stress. If the individual recently had a very challenging spiritual session, then he or she may have a disturbance in his or her energy field. A reiki treatment, meditation session, or performing a grounding technique along with the smudging of sage will most likely have the person back to "normal" in no time. Sometimes only one or two symptoms appear, and you may think you are having a "bad" day. This is true. However, if more extreme symptoms appear, a medical doctor and a spiritual healer should be consulted. If the symptoms start out benign, like a headache and a nightmare, and slowly escalate to bigger and more intense things like loss of memory, hearing voices, or hallucinations, doctors should be consulted. Some of the more severe symptoms include suddenly behaving out of character, sudden loss of energy or total immobilizing fatigue, loss of memory, hearing voices, feeling as if you are being watched all of the time, feeling as if the energy or entity watching you wants to harm you physically, and so on, and a sudden onset of major depression for no apparent reason.

If you experience any of these drastic symptoms or if anyone you know does, especially after a spirit communication session, seek out the help of a professional spiritual healer, energy worker, psychic, and/or a medium for immediate treatment. An extra headache or sore muscle every so often can be remedied. A temporary (mild) feeling of melancholia can be expected, especially when working in traumatic locations or with the ghosts of children. I usually have a really good cry after I make contact with apparitions of children. This is normal. Anything more extreme or violent should be dealt with immediately. Trust me: you will be able to tell the difference. As always, if you do not feel comfortable with a certain location, object, or method of contact, do not do it. The best and most reliable piece of equipment you own is your own perception: always rely on those "gut feelings." They do not lie.

Appendix II
Aromatherapy

Aromatherapy has been used for centuries in conjunction with communication with spirits. The Oracle of Delphi burned sacred incenses to assist in communication with the gods and in the prediction of the future. Bodies were anointed with sacred oils in Egypt in the embalming or mummification process. Essential oils have been used to make perfume, in everyday activities, and for religious ceremonies since ancient times. Now, in my day to day life, I use essential oils in my work as a massage therapist and to enhance my life, too.

I have compiled a list of essential oils that can be blended or used alone. Each specific oil has a use or purpose. It may be ideal for divination, spiritual communication, sleep, purification, etc., or it may be ideal for more than one occupation. As with choosing an amulet or talisman, choosing essential oils is purely subjective. Whichever oil(s) appeals to you is the perfect choice for you. You may want to have one specific oil for protection, one for spirit communication, and one specifically for grounding. For example, you may use cinnamon during a spirit communication session. Then, follow up your grounding exercise with lavender, which is excellent for protection, relaxation and dreams.

BEFORE YOU BEGIN...REMEMBER:

Never ingest any essential oils

Never apply any of the essential oils directly to your skin

Always use a carrier oil. Add 1-2 drops of the desired essential oil into a portable vial of carrier oil (1-2 ounces). Shake to incorporate. Then apply a dab to each wrist, temple, forehead, etc.

Choosing the proper carrier oil for yourself is almost as important as choosing essential oils. Here are three great choices: (1) sweet almond oil is incredible oil. If you really favor it, you may want to consider it for personal aromatherapeutic use only. If you have any type of nut allergy, or if anyone you know and will be working with has a severe nut allergy, then you should definitely avoid the sweet almond oil; (2) grape seed oil works beautifully, and it is the most economical carrier oil available; (3) jojoba oil is absolutely amazing, but can be pricey, especially for the novice. Baby oil (mineral oil) or vegetable oil (aisle five in the grocery store) will only ruin essential oils. Neither of those two oils is recommended for aromatherapy use.

Another option (and a really wise one for a total beginner) is distilled water or isopropyl alcohol in place of a carrier oil. The water or alcohol is placed in a small travel sized spray bottle (3-4 ounce size). You can begin with 1-2 drops of essential oil and use 1-2 more depending on the strength of the scent. Shake well and spray yourself, your amulet or talisman, or even a room if there is residual negative energy in it. Avoid spraying directly in your mouth. A final option is to take a large cotton ball (real cotton, not synthetic fiber) and add one drop of essential oil of your choice to it. Yes, one drop is sufficient. (Remember essential oils are much more subtle than the perfume or cologne from the department store. It is the energy behind the fragrance in the oil that you are working with, not wondering whether the lady five blocks away can smell the blend of oils.)

Then, you can place the cotton ball in your pillow case for dreams and peaceful sleep. Another use for those 35mm film vials is to put the aromatherapeutic cotton balls in them. Now you have mobile aromatherapy. All you need to do is use the proper visualization and inhale the fragrance, wherever you travel. This is not just for supernatural/paranormal activity. I have used a cotton ball with essential lemon oil as a study aid. I would inhale the lemon while studying and bring the cotton ball with me to the test. Just before the test, I would inhale the lemon again. It really works! Lemon is an amazing agent to stimulate the conscious mind and memory.

Before you begin the project of aromatherapy, I strongly advise you to take a formal class. Most massage schools and some community colleges offer beginner classes in aromatherapy. It is usually one weekend, but it will provide you with foundational knowledge of blending, which is priceless. You will only benefit from it. The following is a short list of essential oils, divided into categories like protection, psychic energy, and dreams. Some oils, like jasmine, are multipurpose and can be used for spirituality and peace, while sage is the best possible choice for removing negativity from a room, object, or even residual negative energy from a person. Essential oils have been helping and healing humans and animals for thousands of years.

In addition to their mental and spiritual benefits, they were (and still are) employed to treat a number of physical ailments. Skin problems such as acne or eczema, indigestion, muscle spasms, stiff joints, nausea, headaches, and more are all treated effectively with essential oils. Remember the colonial herbal garden: every household had one, and the lady of the house was the physician in charge of it. Peppermint would have been a vital part of every household in colonial Philadelphia. It is used to treat dermatitis, muscular pain, bronchitis, sinusitis, nausea, headaches, stress, and mental fatigue. It is also used in divination to increase psychic powers. You will find a most amazing world open up to you should you choose to study aromatherapy. I know I am extremely grateful for the knowledge I have acquired on the subject.

I have listed botanical names after common names, because some stores only list under botanical names.

BAY

Laurus Nobilis (also called sweet bay laurel or roman laurel). Bay leaves were used by the ancient Greeks and Romans to crown their victors. Bay is used to increase psychic energy, stimulate the conscious mind, and to increase physical energy. It blends well with pine, juniper, clary sage, lavender, and citrus oils. Herbalist Nicolas Culpeper said this of the Bay Tree: "It resists evil very potently... Neither witch, nor devil, thunder, nor lightening will hurt a man in the place where a Bay Tree lives."

BERGAMOT

Citrus Bergamia. It was named after the Italian city of Bergamo. The ancient Greeks employed it to treat all ailments of the stomach. It is used for peace, especially peaceful sleep or peace while sleeping, and happiness. It blends well with lavender, jasmine, lemon, chamomile, and juniper. If it smells familiar, that is because it is used in Earl Grey tea and some high end perfumes, too.

BLACK PEPPER

Piper Nigrum. This has been used by the Chinese in herbal medicine for over 4,000 years. The ancient Greeks used it to treat all ailments of the stomach. It is used to stimulate the conscious mind, for protection, and for courage. It blends well with frankincense, sandalwood, lavender and floral oils (in very minute amounts).

CAMPHOR

Cinnamomum Camphora. This is a major preventative in the spread of infectious diseases in folk medicine. A lump of camphor was worn around the neck for protection. It is used to increase physical energy, for divination, for purification and cleansing, and for protection.

CHAMOMILE (ROMAN)

Chamamelum Nobile (there is also a German Chamomile variety, but I prefer the Roman). It has been used for over 2000 years by the ancient Egyptians, Moors, Europeans, and Saxons. It is used for meditation, for peace, to promote tranquility, and to achieve tranquil sleep. It blends well with bergamot, jasmine, rose, and lavender. Culpeper had this to say of chamomile: "The bathing with a decoction of chamomile takes away all weariness, eases pains, to what part of the body so ever they be applied."

CINNAMON

Cinnamomum Zeylanicum. It has been used for thousands of years to treat everything from influenza to rheumatism to kidney diseases. It is used for increasing and strengthening psychic powers and psychic awareness. It blends well with ylang ylang, orange, and the oriental oils. Plus a little sprinkle of cinnamon on your toast in the morning makes for a great day!

CLARY SAGE

Salvia Sclarea. This was very popular in the middle ages for digestive issues, kidney complaints, and for use as a general nerve tonic. It is (effectively) used to attain vivid dreams. It blends well with lavender, sandalwood, pine, jasmine, and frankincense.

(USE EXTREME CAUTION: This will really produce vivid dreams! It should only be used when you have become proficient in meditation and concentrative thought. Apply one drop on a (real) cotton ball, take a very small inhale and place it under your pillow, inside the case. Use this along with proper visualization techniques. Clary sage will assist you in attaining the dreams you seek.)

DILL

Anthum Gravolens. This has been used for centuries in Europe as a digestive aid, especially on children for their stomach ailments. It has been used longer in the Scandinavian countries as a culinary herb, too. It is used for purification, for cleansing, to stimulate the conscious mind, and to keep and maintain mental focus. It blends well with mint, caraway, nutmeg, and the spice and the citrus oils. Culpeper says this of dill: "Mercury has the dominion of this plant and therefore, to be sure it strengthens the brain."

EUCALYPTUS

Eucalyptus Globus. This is native to Tasmania. It is a traditional household remedy in Australia for respiratory ailments, fever, and skin disorders. It is used to maintain good health, for purification, and for cleansing. It blends well with thyme, lavender, pine, and lemon.

FRANKINCENSE

Boswellia Carteri. This is a very ancient shrub and was used to treat a wide variety of illnesses, from syphilis to rheumatism to digestion to nervous conditions. It blends well with sandalwood, pine, lavender, mimosa, cinnamon, and orange. It is used when meditating and for spirituality.
(Frankincense was one of the Gifts of the Magi, along with gold and myrrh.)

GARDENIA

Gardenia Jasminoides. The flowers of the gardenia plant are used to flavor tea. Like jasmine, gardenia is used in high end perfumeries all over the world. It is also used for peace (attaining it and keeping it), for love, and for spirituality. It blends well with ylang ylang, jasmine, rose, the spice oils, and the citrus oils.

GARLIC

Allum Sativum. It has been used for thousands of years for just about everything: the treatment of digestive diseases, infestation, skin problems, heart disease, the prevention of gangrene and sepsis, and for protection from vampires. (Vampires were a major threat and fear of those in the 13th, 14th, 15th, and 16th centuries.) It is used for purification and for protection, to maintain physical health, and to increase psychic energies.

GINGER

Zingiber Officinale. This is another very ancient spice, from the east. It was used in China for a variety of things: to treat rheumatism, toothache, malaria, and as a digestive aid. It is used for psychic energy and for physical energy (for stamina with both), and for courage. It blends well with sandalwood, patchouli, rose, lime, and frankincense. (Not to mention, its use in ginger ale and ginger beer.)

HOPS

Humulus Lupulus. It is best known for the brewing of beer, but it has been used in folk medicine for centuries. It was used to treat insomnia, nervous tension, neuralgia, and menstrual ailments. It is used for healing, especially for most sleep ailments, which include falling asleep, staying asleep, and achieving restful sleep. It blends well with pine, hyacinth, the citrus oils, and nutmeg.

IRIS

Iris Pallida (also called Orris). The ancient Greeks and Romans used it to treat bronchitis, cough, and congested headaches. They also used it in perfumes. It is used for psychic awareness, for love, and can be very helpful or instrumental in personal epiphanies or awakenings. It blends well with sandalwood, mimosa, bergamot, clary sage, and the floral oils.

JASMINE

Jasminum Officinale. This is a renaissance plant, or flower. It has been used to treat hepatitis, liver diseases, conjunctivitis, skin ulcers, tumors, headaches, insomnia, and to facilitate childbirth. It is used for love, for the preserving and maintaining of peace, for spirituality, for peaceful sleep, and for psychic dreams. This is one of my favorite essential oils. It blends well with just about all of the oils, or it plays well with others. It can be used alone, in a blend, or as an enhancer to a peaceful sleep blend, meditation blend, and so on.

JUNIPER

Juniperus Comminis. Juniper has a very long history of treating nearly all urinary and bladder diseases, respiratory problems, and it eases gout. It is also used in protection from a psychic attack, for purification, and for healing. It blends well with clary sage, pine, lavender, and the citrus oils. The juniper berries are also used in the distillation of gin.

LAVENDER

Lavandula Angust Folia (also called true lavender). In ancient herbal medicine, it has been used for stomach ailments, toothache(s), relieving faintness (it really does), and as an insect repellent. It is used for the maintaining and preservation of health, for (attaining) love, for peace, and for sleep—especially peaceful dreaming. It also increases the powers of the conscious mind. It blends well with many of the essential oils, especially the citrus oils, the floral oils, and patchouli. In many aspects, lavender is like jasmine as it is a universal go-to oil. If you want to boost the power of your essential oil blend, you can add to the intensity of the energy of the oil by adding a drop of lavender. For example, if you have a sleep blend, add a drop of lavender and you will have a sleep blend with a booster.

LEMON

Citrus Limon. Traditionally, this has been a cure all, especially with infectious diseases, scurvy, and arthritis. It is used for the maintaining of physical health, for healing, for physical energy (to increase it), for protection, for purification, and for cleansing. It blends well with lavender, orange, rose, juniper, chamomile, and myrrh.

LIME

Citrus Aurantifolia. Traditionally, this was the substitute for lemon in ancient herbal medicine. It is used for psychic energy (to strengthen it), for protection, and for purification. It blends well with lavender, neroli, clary sage, and the citrus oils.

MIMOSA

Acacia Deal Bata. Mimosa is another native Australian tree. It is used mainly as an antiseptic and an astringent. It is primarily used for achieving (and remembering) psychic dreams. It blends well with lavender, ylang ylang, the floral oils, and the spice oils.

MUGWORT

Artemesia Vulgaris. This is a very ancient herb. It is believed that Saint John the Baptist wore mugwort leaves around his waist when he went into the wilderness. In ancient herbal medicine, it was used to treat hysteria, epilepsy, and to control fever. It was worn around the neck as an amulet (charm) to repel all evil. It is used for psychic awareness (to increase and intensify it), for meditation (to have stronger powers of concentrative thought), and for dreams (all types—prophetic, vivid and psychic). It has also been used in astral projection (to aid in the process of it) and protects the physical body during it. It blends well with patchouli, lavender, jasmine, pine, sage, and clary sage. Culpeper had this to say of mugwort; "It is an herb of Venus... The herb itself or juice is a special remedy upon the overmuch taking of opium..."
(*Mugwort is a very powerful and potent herb and not to be played with, underestimated, or taken lightly. It should never be used by pregnant women or children. It is not recommended for the beginner or amateur aromatherapist. Caution should always be taken with mugwort.)

MYRRH

Commiphora Myrrha. This ancient shrub, like frankincense, pre-dates Jesus Christ. It has been used to treat arthritis, menstrual problems, asthma, all cold symptoms, and even leprosy. It is used for meditation (for the calming and stilling of the mind), for healing (mental and physical), and for spirituality. It blends well with frankincense, patchouli, rose, lavender, mint, and the spice oils. Myrrh was one of the Gifts of the Magi, along with frankincense and gold. It is very rare to have access to true/pure myrrh essential oil. The myrrh out there is either synthetic or synthetic blend. However, there are some good synthetic blends. You just have to seek them out. They are very expensive.

NIAOULI

Melaleuca Viridflora. It has been used for aches and pains, for respiratory infections, cuts and skin infections, and even to purify drinking water. It is used primarily for protection and for healing. It blends well with jasmine, lavender, and eucalyptus.

NUTMEG

Myristica Fragrams. In herbal medicine, nutmeg was used as a digestive aid and for kidney disorders. It was also used in candle and soap making. It is used for physical energy (to increase it), for psychic energy, and for psychic awareness (to intensify it). It blends well with orange, bay, lime, and the spice oils.

ORANGE

Citrus sinensis. Chinese herbal medicine used orange to treat all symptoms of the cold, anorexia, and malignant breast sores. It is for joy (to achieve and attain it), for purification, for physical energy (to increase it), and for psychic energy. It blends well with lavender, lemon, myrrh, clary sage, and the spice oils. Children respond well to orange essential oil. It can be used across the board with them for treating headaches, lethargy, and even nightmares.

PATCHOULI

Pogostemon Cablin. It has been used to prevent the spread of infectious diseases, to treat headaches, nausea, and various stomach ailments. It is also used to scent linens and clothing. It is used for physical energy (for stamina), and for protecting the physical body in times of stress and distress. Patchouli is earth charged. Its scent is from the earth and its properties are from the earth, too. It is excellent for assistance in all grounding exercises, routines, and rituals. It is highly effective in warding off a psychic attack and the treatment of symptoms of a psychic attack (if you are a victim of one). It blends well with sandalwood, rose, bergamot, lavender, myrrh, and clary sage. Patchouli is like licorice and the Grateful Dead: there are no substitutions, facsimiles, or imitations. It is the only thing that does what it does. Those of us who love it love it whole heartedly, and those who do not—well, you get the general idea. It has the most amazing energy, and it would be a shame if it was overlooked because of its overuse in the 1960s.

PEPPERMINT

Mentha Piperita. Mints were cultivated in ancient Egypt and China. It was used mostly as a digestive aid, but also alleviates headaches, symptoms of pregnancy, and lethargy. It is used for purification and for stimulating the conscious mind, especially the memory. It blends well with lavender, lemon, and eucalyptus.

PINE

Pinus Sylvestris (also called scotch pine). Baths were taken with boiled pine needles to relieve nervous tension, circulatory disorders, slow-healing wounds, arthritis, and skin disorders. It was also used to repel lice and fleas. It is used for healing and for purification (especially rooms and amulets), for protection, and physical energy. It blends well with sage, lavender, lemon, juniper, and eucalyptus.

ROSE

Rosa Centifolia (also called cabbage rose). Healing powers of the rose are ancient and worked on a wide variety of illnesses, such as digestive disorders, headaches, circulatory problems, fever, eye infections, and skin issues. It is used primarily for love (attaining and maintaining), but also for peace and, of course, beauty (to attract more into your life). It blends well with patchouli, myrrh, jasmine, bergamot, mimosa, clary sage, and chamomile.

SAGE

Salvia Officinalis (also called common sage). The ancient Romans called it a sacred herb. It was used for a wide variety of treatments, such as for respiratory infections, menstrual difficulties, and digestive disorders. It is used for the strengthening of the conscious mind, for wisdom (attaining), and especially the removal of all negative energies. It blends well with lavender, lemon, and the citrus oils. Culpeper had this to say about sage: "Sage drank with vinegar hath been of good use in time of the plague at all times."

SANDALWOOD

Santalum Album. It is over 4,000 years old, and it is one of the oldest perfume materials in the world. It was also used as an incense in holy temples. It is used for meditation, for spirituality, for healing, and for the purification of large rooms or areas. It blends well with rose, black pepper, bergamot, patchouli, mimosa, jasmine, and myrrh.

SPEARMINT

Mentha Spicata. The ancient Greeks used spearmint in bath water and to treat nausea and indigestion. It is used in healing, for protection (general protection from evil), and for protection during sleep. It blends well with lavender, jasmine, and is very often used with peppermint. Culpeper had this to say of spearmint: "Applied with salt, it helps with the biting of a mad dog."

THYME

Thymus Vulgaris (also called common thyme). The ancient Egyptians and Hippocrates used it to prevent the spread of infectious diseases and in the embalming process. It is used for courage, for the conscious mind (strengthening of), and for overall general health. It blends well with bergamot, lemon, lavender, and pine

YLANG YLANG

Cananga Odorata, var. Genesina. It was used for the treatment of skin diseases, for the prevention of fever, and to encourage hair growth. It is used for peace (attainment and keeping) and for love (strengthening and maintaining). It blends well with jasmine, bergamot, rose, and mimosa.

PUTTING IT ALL TOGETHER

Now that you have all the components, how do you put everything together for the optimum result? It may seem a bit overwhelming, especially if all of this is new to you. All it takes is a little practice and preparation. Think of it as one of those fabulous vegetable stir-fry dishes that has about twenty different vegetables, and you only order it in the restaurant because you think it is way too difficult to do at home. Well, it really is not difficult at all. It just takes some preparation, and I am going to guide you through it step by step. Let's begin.

First, preparation is the key. You have to decide which essential oils and what method(s) you are going to use. I suggest you start with three or four spray bottles (travel size) with distilled water or isopropyl alcohol as a carrier and three or four essential oils. If you can do four, that would be the best option. Bottle one should contain sage. No matter what other oils you choose or use, you should always have sage oil. It is the best purifier that I have ever used. Bottle two should be oil that specializes in psychic energy, like cinnamon, lime, ginger, or nutmeg. Bottle three should contain oil that is for peace, peaceful sleep, and so on, like bergamot, jasmine, lavender, rose, or ylang ylang. Finally, bottle four should be a cleansing, protection bottle with lemon, eucalyptus, juniper, or pine. As you gain experience in blending and aromatherapy in general, you can make a peaceful blend of 2-3 oils. However, you should always have that single bottle of sage.

Now that you have you essential oil bottles, next thing you may want to have with you is an amulet or talisman. It can be anything, from the cross you wear around your neck everyday to a specific crystal or quartz you only use for spiritual work. Next, choose your equipment. If you are going low tech, that is just as effective as taking the high-tech toys. It is all very subjective, and totally dependent on your level of comfort and ease with your equipment. I am very low tech. I either wear my mother's agate ring or my aquamarine ring, depending on how I feel that day, and take my pendulum. In terms of equipment, my 35mm camera with 400sp film is my companion. Sometimes, I bring along a mini tape recorder (left over from my student days). That is it. I prefer simplicity. However, I am in no way anti-technology. It is extremely cool to see a spirit's energy moving on a monitor. Ideally, I try to hook up with the high-tech people, so we have the best of both worlds.

Now, you have your essential oil sprays, your amulet, and your choice of equipment. The next step is your preparation ritual. This preparation exercise can be simple and take no more than 15 minutes. First, take all of your equipment—amulet, camera, and so on—and spray the equipment (or the air above it: Do not soak any sensitive electronic equipment!) with your sage. A quick general spritz will neutralize the energy of the objects. Put the amulet on (if it is a necklace, ring, etc.).

At this time you can do the 10-minute meditation technique mentioned previously. When finished meditating, take your bottle of psychic energy spray and spray the air directly in front of you. Walk through the mist and visualize your psychic passages opening and receptive to energy. Now you are ready for spiritual work. Take both of the sage and psychic energy bottles with you. If at any time during your spiritual "field trip" you feel threatened, do a grounding exercise immediately and spray the sage. Visualize the negative energy disappearing and only positive energy and white light existing. Also, if the energy feels blocked, you can spray the psychic energy and visualize open channels of communication.

The session is finished. The next step is grounding and protecting. Before you leave the haunted site, you can do one of the simple grounding techniques, like stomping and visualizing the energies returning to where they came from. When you return home, ease into your normal routine or relax and watch a DVD. Take the cleansing spray and spritz your amulet and equipment, again a super fine mist, not a soaking. Visualize the energy being neutralized. Spray the air directly in front of you and walk through the mist, visualizing all residual energy dissipating. While showering, you can visualize the energy going down the drain. Finally, you can spray yourself with the peaceful spray (and your pillow, too) while asking for positive, peaceful dreams. You can also do the meditation technique while drifting off to sleep, if you choose to do so.

If you take the proper precautions and follow through on the grounding techniques, your spirit experiences will be quite rewarding. Happy hunting and happy haunting!

Appendix III
Glossary Of Terms

AMULET – also called a talisman; a symbolic object infused with energy that protects the wearer from harm, rings and necklaces being the most popular forms of amulet/talisman

ANOMALY – an occurrence or happening for which there is no "normal" explanation

APPARITION – the projection or manifestation of a paranormal being

CHANNELING – the procedure of bringing information directly from the spirit world

CLAIRALIENCE – also called clear smelling; the process in which an individual(s) smells an odor from the spirit world; examples: tobacco, flowers or perfume

CLAIRAUDIENCE – also called clear hearing; the ability to hear sounds, voices and so on from the spirit world

CLAIRSENTIENCE – also called clear sensing, psychic perception; used by a medium to sense information from the spirit world without seeing or hearing

CLAIRVOYANCE – also called clear seeing; seeing in the mind's eye; the seeing of spirits, scenes and any other visual information from the spirit world

DIVINATION – the procedure or technique in which future events are revealed to an individual through spiritual means; some of the most popular forms being the reading of tarot cards, scrying, the use of a Ouija or spirit board, reading tea leaves, numerology, and the use of a pendulum

DOWSING – the procedure of using of 2 rods to locate substances, energies or energy fields, often with the use of a pendulum suspended from a chain; one of the most popular methods for locating water

ELECTRO MAGNETIC FIELD – also called EMF; anything that uses electricity or generates a magnetic field

ENTITY – a disembodied being; a ghost or a spirit

ELECTRONIC VOICE PHENOMENA – also called EVP; an utterance or sound not heard as it is spoken, but audible when the recording is played back

GHOST – a spirit who may or may not have been human or animal; may appear semi-transparent (*animal ghosts possibly being family pets or omens of future events)

HAUNTING – the repeated appearance of ghosts, spirits, or poltergeists, generally falling into one of two categories:

INTELLIGENT HAUNTINGS – situations occurring when the entity in question is aware of the presence of humans and can (and sometimes does) interact with them

RESIDUAL HAUNTINGS – situations occurring when the entity in question is oblivious to observers; more like a psychic recording of an event (traumatic or other)

KINESTHESIA – a sensation in which a psychic or medium feels the presence of a spirit

MANIFESTATION – also called materialization; the appearance of an entity seen as it is materializing

MEDIUM – a person who has the ability or gift to communicate with the dead

NECROMANCY – the art and practice of communicating with the dead, tools such as a Ouija Board or spirit board often being employed to obtain knowledge regarding the future

POLTERGEIST – also called a noisy ghost; truly rare form of haunting, where random objects are moved and sounds, sometimes speech, are produced by unseen entities who crave attention, a child or adolescent usually being at the center of these phenomena

PRE-COGNITION – the ability to know events, conversations, and so on ahead of time

PSYCHO KINESIS – also called Telekinesis; the paranormal phenomena in which objects are moved solely by the power of the mind

RETRO-COGNITION – the phenomenon in which knowledge of things from the past comes to an individual, but not by normal means

SCRYING – a popular divination technique in which a crystal ball or any reflective device, such as a bowl of water, can be used: images of the future and/or the past are seen when gazing into said device

SÉANCE – event or happening that occurs when a group of individuals attempt to contact the spirit world; usually done through the assistance of a medium

SHADOW GHOSTs – also called Shadow Figures or even Shadow People; very dark, human figures most often sighted in one's peripheral vision, appearing more like human silhouettes (sightings of shadow ghost's facial features being very rare)

SKOTOGRAPH – spirit-produced photographs on raw photo paper without the use of a camera

SPIRIT – the essence of a person that moves from the physical body to the ethereal

SPIRIT PHOTOGRAPHY – the procedure of capturing spirit forms in photographs, whether intentional or non-intentional

WRAITH – a semi-transparent image of an individual, which appears very shortly after that person's death

Bibliography

Text Sources

Adams III, Charles J. *Philadelphia Ghost Stories.* Reading, PA: Exeter House Books, 2001.

Buckland, Raymond. *Doors to Other Worlds: A Practical Guide to Communicating with Spirits.* St. Paul, MN: Llewellyn Publications, 1997.

Colimore, Edward. *Philadelphia Inquirer's Walking Tours of Philadelphia.* Philadelphia, PA: Camino Books, 2001-2008.

Culpeper's Complete Herbal: A Book of Natural Remedies for Ancient Ills. Ware, Hertfordshire, Great Britain: Wordsworth Reference; Nashville: Cumberland House, Wordsworth Editions, Ltd., 1995.

Cunningham, Scott. *Magical Aromatherapy.* St. Paul, MN: Llewellyn Publications, 1989.

George, Alice L. *Old City Philadelphia: Cradle of American Democracy.* Charleston, SC: Arcadia Publishing. 2003.

Graham, Robert. *"Philadelphia Inns and Taverns from 1774-1780".* Research paper, University of Pennsylvania. 1952.

Hauck, Dennis William. *The National Directory Haunted Places, Ghostly Abodes, Sacred Sites, UFO Landings, and Other Supernatural Locations.* New York: Penguin Publications, 1994.

Horman, Lynn M. and Thomas Reilly. *Visiting Turn of the Century Philadelphia.* Charleston, SC: Arcadia Publishing, 1999.

Kyriakodis, Harry. *Philadelphia's Lost Waterfront.* Charleston, SC: The History Press, 2011.

Lake, Matt. *Weird Pennsylvania.* Edited by Mark Sceurman and Mark Moran. New York: Sterling Publishing, 2005.

Lawless, Julia. *The Encyclopedia of Essential Oils: The Complete Guide to the Use of Aromatic Oils in Aromatherapy, Herbalism, Health and Well Being.* Hammersmith, London, Great Britain: Thorsons, 1992.

Mabbot, T.O., ed. *The Selected Poetry and Prose of Edgar Allan Poe.* The Modern Literary College Edition. New York: Random House, 1951.

McMichael, George, ed. *Anthology of American Literature: 1. Colonial through Romantic.* New York: Macmillan Publishing, 1985.

Nesbitt, Mark and Patty A. Wilson. *Haunted Pennsylvania: Ghosts and Strange Phenomena of the Keystone State.* Mechanicsburg, PA: Stack Pole Books, 2006.

Nesbitt, Mark. *Big Book of Pennsylvania Ghost Stories.* Mechanicsburg, PA: Stack Pole Books, 2008.

Sarro, Katherine. *Philadelphia Haunts: Eastern State Penitentiary, Fort Mifflin, & Other Ghostly Haunts.* Atglen, PA: Schiffer Books, 2008.

Schlosser, S.E. *Spooky Pennsylvania: Tales of Hauntings, Strange Happenings, and Other Local Lore.* Guilford, CT: Insider's Guide, 2007.

Watson, John F. *Annals of Philadelphia in Olden Time.* Vols. 1, 2 and 3. Philadelphia: Edwin Stewart, 1900.

Westcott, Thomas. *The Historic Mansions and Buildings of Philadelphia: With Some Notice of Their Owners and Occupants.* Philadelphia: 1877. Reprinted. Salem, MA: Higginson Book Company.

Wood, Maureen and Ron Kolek. *A Ghost A Day.* Avon, MA: Adams Media, 2010.

Website Resources

www.americanhistory.org
www.angelfire.com/ghostsofphiladelphia
www.delco.com
www.ghosttheory.com
www.ghostvillage.com
www.hauntsandhistory.blogspot.com
www.historicghost.com
www.philalandmarks.org
www.ushistory.org
www.newhopehistoricalsociety.org